CHRISTMAS COOKIES

CHRISTMAS
COOKIES

MORE THAN 60 CUTE RECIPES FOR
FUN FESTIVE BAKES

with an introduction by
HANNAH MILES

RYLAND PETERS & SMALL
LONDON • NEW YORK

Senior Designers Toni Kay and
Sonya Nathoo
Editor Sarah Vaughan
Head of Production Patricia Harrington
Creative Director Leslie Harrington
Editorial Director Julia Charles

Indexer Stephen Blake

First published in 2020. This edition
published in 2024 by
Ryland Peters & Small
20–21 Jockey's Fields
London WC1R 4BW
and
341 East 116th St
New York NY 10029
www.rylandpeters.com

10 9 8 7 6 5 4 3 2 1

Text copyright © Brontë Aurell,
Susannah Blake, Chloe Coker, Linda
Collister, Hannah Miles, Annie Rigg,
Will Torrent and Ryland Peters & Small
2020, 2024
Design and photographs copyright
© Ryland Peters & Small 2020, 2024

ISBN: 978-1-78879-641-5

Printed in China

A CIP record for this book is available
from the British Library.
US Library of Congress Cataloging-in-
Publication Data has been applied for.

Notes:
• Both British (Metric) and American
(Imperial plus US cup) measurements
are included in these recipes for your
convenience, however it is important
to work with one set of measurements
and not alternate between the two
within a recipe.
• All spoon measurements are level unless
otherwise specified.
• All eggs are medium (UK) or large (US),
unless specified as large, in which case
US extra-large should be used.
• Ovens should be preheated to the
specified temperatures. If you are using
a fan-assisted oven, adjust temperatures
according to the manufacturer's
instructions.
• When a recipe calls for the grated zest
of citrus fruit, buy unwaxed fruit.

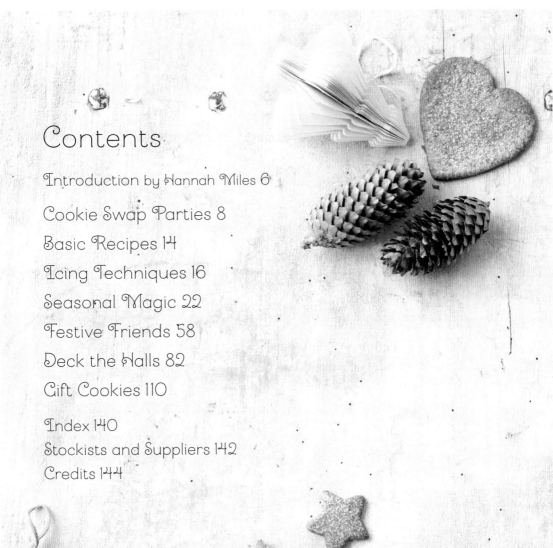

Contents

Introduction by Hannah Miles

Christmas is the perfect time for festive baking – take time to celebrate the best of the season by making delicious home-made treats to delight friends and family. Whether you are hosting a cookie swap at home, or want to take gifts to those you are visiting, cookies are a quick, easy and versatile option.

Make the most of time with children over the festive season – they love to bake and there is nothing nicer than baking cookies for Santa together or helping them to prepare thoughtful (and economical!) home-made gifts for their school classmates. Having batches of fresh cookies prepared ahead are perfect standbys for unexpected Christmas visitors or hungry little tummies.

Cookies also make ideal gifts as they are simple to prepare and taste better than anything you might find at the supermarket. Using general store cupboard ingredients, most only take about 10–15 minutes to bake! In this book you'll find all my cookie swap favourites, alongside delicious ideas by other experienced bakers – from tree decorations and smiling Santas to highly decorated iced cookies that make pretty gifts once wrapped in clear cellophane. There is a wide variety of simple ideas such as cookies disguised as candies, or if you are feeling adventurous, try your hand at making an entire mini gingerbread village, certain to 'wow' your guests.

Whatever cookies are your favourite, don your apron, find your festive spirit and bake wonderful Christmas cookies today.

Cookie Swap Parties

One of my favourite things to do at Christmas is to host a cookie swap party. They are a chance to meet up with lots of friends or family in one go at a busy time of year, and a way of cheap and cheerfully gifting, and a fun 'event' that most can enjoy any time of day. The basic idea is to invite your friends and family to your home and each guest brings their favourite type of home-made cookie. Everyone then swaps their cookies and, having arrived a large selection of one cookie, you go home with the same number, but of all different varieties! It's the perfect way to end up with a delicious array of cookies for Christmas. Cookie swap parties do not need much preparation – I just put on a large pan of mulled wine and serve a few Christmas nibbles, but the main focus should be the cookies and the creative ways they can be displayed, or even decorated.

Guests can bring several dozen cookies that can be shared out, or they can bring enough ready-wrapped bags of cookies so that there is one for each guest to take home. If you don't want to make people bring cookies, why not have a baking party where you provide each guest with a basic cookie dough to which they can add flavouring and candies of their choosing, and then bake them all together – as long as you don't mind the washing-up! You could also host a cookie party coffee morning.

How to Host a Cookie Swap Party

First you need to decide on a date and place for your party and choose whether to have a theme (see page 10).

Next, invite your guests – take the time to write invitations that explain the concept of a cookie party in case your friends have not been to one before. The idea is that your friends should pick their favourite cookie recipe and bake batches of these to bring to the party. You need to tell them the number of cookies to bring so that they have enough to exchange with all the other guests. You can either ask them to bring the cookies all together or to pack then into individual bags so that there is one bag of cookies for each guest. It's important to make sure that you give clear instructions on how many cookies you need – everyone to bring 2 or 3 dozen is generally what is expected, but this will depend on how many guests are coming to the party. Always have a few extra on standby in case there are any mix ups.

It's a nice idea to encourage guests to write up the recipe so that it can be shared (unless it is a treasured family secret!). This way, not only do your guests get batches of tasty cookies, they will have new recipes for their cook books so that they can bake the cookies they like again. You could also ask people to send you the recipes the week before so that you can compile them into a recipe sheet or booklet for all your guests that will make a memento of the event.

Don't forget to enquire if people have any allergies, and let the other guests know if this is the case as it is important to make sure that there are no allergy concerns on the day.

Spend time planning decorations and music for your party. You could also prepare going-home bags or favours for your guests if you want to make it extra special – a simple cookie cutter tied with pretty ribbon is one of my favourite gifts for cookie lovers.

It is important to think about some savories to serve at your party as you need to counter the sugar from the cookies. Cheese straws, simple canapes, crisps and nuts all take no time to prepare. I love warm olives, roasted for about 5–8 minutes in a moderate oven.

Think about what drinks to serve. Glasses of milk to have with the cookies bring back childhood memories, but other options could be hot chocolate, festive mulled wine or even mulled cider. Or, why not design a signature cocktail to match your party theme!

During the party, I like to ask everyone to tell the other guests about the origins of their recipe and how to make it. If you want the party to have a little light hearted competition, get people to secretly vote for the tastiest, best decorated, most festive and the most original cookie of the evening and have prizes for the winning bakers.

If you have time, send thank you cards after the event, which I always think is a nice touch.

Party Theme Ideas

Whilst just hosting a general cookie swap party is perfectly enjoyable, you may want to give your guests a theme to add some extra creativity and excitement. If you host an annual cookie party then guests will look forward to hearing your theme, so be creative. My favourite ideas are:

ROUND THE WORLD COOKIE PARTY

Give each of your guests a different country as their theme and then each person brings a traditional cookie from that country. You might have Anzac biscuits from Australia, linzer cookies from Austria, snickerdoodles from America and custard creams from England. To decorate your party room you can use flags, and if your guests are feeling particularly creative, they could bring items from their theme country for the cookie display.

DECORATED COOKIE PARTY

Task your friends with decoratively icing their cookies, or alternatively, ask everyone to bring plain cookies and ice them together – for this you would need to provide bowls of royal and glacé icing, food colouring, icing bags and nozzles/tips, and plenty of sweets/candies for decoration. For inspiration, print out decorating ideas and place them on the tables.

COLOUR THEMED PARTY

Ask your guests to bake cookies within a colour theme – for Christmas you could pick red and green, and decorate your room with red and green table cloths, Christmas crackers and paper chains. If your cookie swaps become a hit and you host one at other events, try pink and blue for a baby shower swap, or black and white for a bridal shower. Or theme a party as a 'rainbow' and ask for multi-coloured cookies.

SECRET SANTA COOKIE PARTY

If you fancy challenging your friends give them each a secret recipe to cook for the party, or get everyone to provide a recipe and swap them for another person to bake and bring along.

CHOCOLATE COOKIE PARTY

Ask your guests to bring cookies made with chocolate, and serve hot chocolate with the cookies for an extra treat for chocaholics.

CHRISTMAS TREE DECORATIONS

Ask your guests to bring cookies that can be hung, so that everyone can take home pretty cookies to decorate their own trees. See pages 84–109 for suggestions.

CHRISTMAS JUMPER/SWEATER PARTY

Why not suggest that your guests come wearing their favourite festive tops and decorate your cookies as a Christmas outfit.

FESTIVE FRIENDS

Theme your party around Christmas characters so each guest is given inspiration for their cookie – reindeer, penguins, Santa etc. See pages 60 –81 for suggestions you could use.

Packaging and Display Ideas

PACKAGING

There are many different packaging ideas for your cookies. If you are not asking your guests to bring their cookies already packaged, as host, you will need to provide gift wrapping. This is the bit I love as I am forever collecting ribbons, boxes and other decorative items to use for my baking. These are a few suggestions:

- *Cake boxes lined with festive tissue paper*
- *Large glass or Kilner jars*
- *Biscuit/cookie or cake tins*
- *Clear plastic bags or cellophane with ribbons*
- *Make giant cones with decorative cardboard*
- *Popcorn buckets or pretty paper candy bags*
- *If available cheaply, you could provide each guest with a festive serving tray or platter so that they can take their cookies home displayed, covering them with clear clingfilm/plastic wrap*

You may want to provide a selection of the above so everyone can be creative. Add lots of ribbons, stickers and gift tags so that guests can. Even brown paper is made special with stripy twine or patterned rubber and ink stamps. You could also provide your guests with plain boxes and allow time for them to be decorated, and then award a small prize for the best decorated box.

Alternatively, ask your guests to bring their own packaging or containers for taking their cookies home. This will make life easier for you.

TABLE DISPLAYS

The highlight of your party should be the display table – lay a pretty cloth and adorn the table with festive decorations. If your guests are bringing loose cookies, cover your table with cake stands so that each guest can use one each. It is good to use a variety of heights so that all cookies can be admired. Make sure that you have room on the table, or have another table spare, for serving savoury nibbles, or hand these round separately.

The Italians have a wonderful tradition of cookie gifting tables, mainly used at weddings, where you bake a multitude of cookies in different colours and styles, and display them on a large table in patterns. Each person is then given a gift box to pack full of cookies to take home. You could use this idea for your party, and as each guest arrives, ask them to add their cookies in patterns and lines on the table.

Think about adding those festive extras such as bunting saying "Cookie Swap" or tying baubles on ribbons and hang them across the room. Table flowers can add a special touch – fresh flowers or even a simple vases of holly will do nicely. If you have the time, making paper chains with children is another lovely way to decorate the room. And don't forget to take a group photo of all your guests and their cookies. You may like to use the photo on the invite to your next cookie party.

However you decide to arrange your party, the most important thing is to spend time with friends and share your love of cookies.

Basic Recipes

Here are two delicious basic cookie dough recipes that can be used time and again throughout the festive period

Vanilla Cookie Dough

This dough makes lovely buttery cookies. It is delicious as it is, but to make them chocolate, replace 60 g/½ cup of the flour with unsweetened cocoa powder.

250 g/2 sticks unsalted butter, at room temperature
125 g/²/₃ cup unrefined caster/superfine sugar
1 egg yolk
1 teaspoon pure vanilla extract
250 g/2½ cups plain/all-purpose flour
125 g/1¼ cups self-raising/rising flour
pinch of salt

Cream the butter and sugar together until light and creamy. Whisk/beat in the egg yolk and vanilla extract. Sift in the flours and salt, mixing everything together until the mixture forms a soft dough. Stop mixing as soon as the flour is incorporated, as you do not want to overwork the dough. Wrap the dough in clingfilm/plastic wrap and chill in the fridge for at least 1 hour.

On a flour-dusted surface, roll out the dough. Cut out cookies with a cutter of your choice, re-rolling as necessary. Place on a lined baking sheet and chill in the fridge for 30 minutes.

Preheat the oven to 200°C (400°F) Gas 6.

Bake in the preheated oven for 12–16 minutes until the cookies are golden.

Gingerbread Cookie Dough

This versatile recipe makes a gently spiced dough with a hint of citrus, but you can change the quantities of spices to suit your taste.

125 g/1 stick unsalted butter
100g/½ cup dark soft brown sugar
2 tablespoons water
2 tablespoons golden syrup/light corn syrup
1 tablespoon treacle/molasses
250 g/2½ cups plain/all-purpose flour
½ teaspoon bicarbonate of soda/baking soda
100 g /1 cup self-raising/self-rising flour
1 tablespoon ground ginger
2 teaspoons ground cinnamon
2 teaspoons mixed spice/apple pie spice
finely grated zest of 1 orange or lemon (optional)

Put the butter, sugar, water, syrup and molasses in a heavy-based saucepan and melt over a low heat, stirring occasionally. Remove from the heat and leave to cool for a few minutes.

Sift the flours, baking soda and the spices into a large bowl and add the citrus zest, if using.

Make a well in the dry ingredients and pour in the liquid mixture. Gently stir, until the mixture comes together to form a soft dough.

On a flour-dusted surface, roll out the dough. Cut out cookies with a cutter of your choice, re-rolling as necessary. Place on a lined baking sheet and chill in the fridge for 30 minutes.

Preheat the oven to 200°C (400°F) Gas 6.

Bake in the preheated oven for 8–12 minutes until the cookies are golden.

Icing Techniques

There are two main ways to cover a cookie: flooding it with royal icing or covering it with rolled fondant icing (sugar paste). Both methods produce lovely results and are often interchangeable, depending on your personal preference.

Royal Icing

This is a traditional recipe for royal icing that's perfect for decorating cookies in whichever pattern or colour you choose. Always make sure your mixing bowl is clean and free of grease. If you prefer to use an egg-free icing that provides similar results, try the Glacé Icing recipe to the right.

2 extra-large egg whites
450 g /3¼ cups icing/confectioners' sugar
2 teaspoons lemon juice

Put the egg white and lemon juice in a large, clean, mixing bowl. Slowly add the icing/confectioners' sugar, mixing it gently by hand or on a slow speed in food processor until incorporated. Increase the speed to medium and beat the icing for 5–10 minutes until it turns bright white and glossy and holds its shape like a stiff meringue.

Glacé Icing

250 g/1¾ cup icing/confectioners' sugar
2–3 tablespoons water or lemon juice

Sift the icing sugar into a bowl and, using a balloon whisk, gradually stir in enough water or lemon juice to make a smooth icing that will coat the back of a spoon. Add more water or juice for a runnier icing.

OUTLINING COOKIES

When piping icing, make sure the top of the piping bag is tightly folded down so that the bag is taut. The pressure should be coming from the top of the bag, so squeeze the bag from the top, not the middle, using your dominant hand. You may want to use the fingers of your other hand to steady the bag. The purpose of the outline is to create a barrier to hold the flooding icing on the cookie. With your first few projects, you may want to use a wider nozzle/tip (Wilton size 4) to make a thicker barrier so that the icing is less likely to overflow. As you get more confident, you will be able use a narrow nozzle/tip (Wilton size 1–2), which gives a more subtle outline.

When outlining the cookie, pipe as close to the edge of the cookie as possible. Hold the bag at a 45-degree angle, apply even pressure, and move the bag steadily along the cookie.

For best results, lift the tip off the cookie and allow the icing to fall, rather than dragging the tip along the surface of the cookie.

Don't worry if it goes wrong: the icing will be fairly elastic and you will be able to move it with a cocktail stick/toothpick or use a damp paintbrush to tidy your icing. Although the neater the better, don't worry if your outline is not perfect, provided there are no gaps in it.

Once the cookie is flooded, you won't notice any minor imperfections. Leave the outline to dry for a few minutes before flooding the cookie (see opposite).

FLOODING WITH ICING

With this method, the icing dries very hard to give the cookie a smooth, professional finish. It is a more complicated and time-consuming method than using rolled fondant, but it produces beautiful results. This is the method used by many professional cookie makers.

Flooded cookies are made in two stages: first they are outlined with piping icing and then they are flooded with flooding icing. Both types of icing are made from the same basic royal icing recipe (see opposite). As a guide, you will need one-third of the icing in each flooded recipe to outline the cookies and the other two-thirds to flood them.

Use the icing as it is to outline the cookies, but for flooding you will need to thin it with a little water until it reaches the consistency of emulsion paint. Add water a teaspoonful at a time until you get the right consistency.

Spread some icing onto the cookie, keeping it away from the edges. Spread enough icing onto the cookie so that it looks generously covered, but not so much that it overflows.

Use a round-bladed knife to guide the icing so that it floods any gaps.

Once you have flooded the cookie, check the surface for any air bubbles and pop them with a cocktail stick/toothpick. Note that if you start flooding your cookies and realize that the consistency is not quite right, it is better to stop and fix it rather than persevering, as the results will never be satisfactory.

  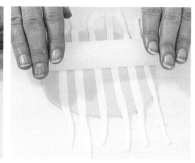

COVERING WITH ROLLED FONDANT

Rolled fondant, also available as ready-to-roll icing, is perfect for decorating cakes and cookies. It is sold in most good cake shops, supermarkets or online baking stockists (see page 142).

Using rolled fondant provides a very quick and easy way to decorate cakes and cookies and is ideal for children, as it is not as complicated as flooding with royal icing. If the icing does not stick, and you have no edible glue, use a little corn syrup or sugar syrup made from dissolving sugar and warm water on a 1:1 ratio and brushing over the cookies.

Work the icing between your fingers until it is pliable. Try not to use your palms, as they will make the icing sticky. To colour the icing, put some food colouring on a cocktail stick/toothpick and put it in the icing, then knead the icing until the colour is fully blended with no streaks.

Roll the icing out on a clean work surface dusted with icing/confectioners' sugar to a 3 mm/⅛ inch thickness. Then cut the icing into your chosen shapes using a cookie cutter, or a sharp knife. If the icing is not too dry, it will stick to the cookie or cake; alternatively, brush the cookie with edible glue using a damp brush. Attach the icing to the cookie or cake. If the cookie has spread a little in the oven, lightly roll over the icing to stretch it right to the edges of the cookie or cake. Finally, run your finger around the edge of the icing to smooth it on for a perfect finish.

POLKA DOTS

Polka-dot rolled fondant looks great on iced cookies. To make polka-dot icing, roll out some white icing as normal. Then roll some small balls of coloured icing between your fingers and squash these down onto the white icing using your thumb. When all the balls are in place, gently roll over the icing with a rolling pin to incorporate the dots into the white icing.

STRIPES

To make stripes, roll out some coloured icing and some white icing to a 3 mm/⅛ inch thickness. Cut the white icing into thin strips and lay them over the coloured icing. Roll over the strips to incorporate.

BOWS

Once you have learnt to make the icing bows, you can use them on all sorts of different cakes and cookies.

Dust a work surface with icing/confectioners' sugar. Make some polka-dot rolled fondant using the technique on page 20. Cut out squares of rolled fondant the same size as the cookies.

To make a bow, cut out a strip of red rolled fondant about 1 cm/3/8 inch wide and twice the length that you would like the bow to be. Take one end and fold it into the middle, making sure that the curl stands open (you can use the end of a paintbrush to support it). Fold in the other half so that the ends meet in the middle.

Lay the bow on another, slightly thinner, strip of rolled fondant. Fold in the ends of this strip and turn the bow over. Finally, gently squeeze the sides to shape the bow.

To make the ribbon tails, cut a strip of rolled fondant 1 cm/3/8 inch wide. Cut it in half and cut little triangles in the ends. Attach the strips to the centre of the cookie and stick the bow on top.

Seasonal Magic

Iced Mitten Cookies

Make adorable mitten cookies and tie them in pairs for a fun gift.
If you do not have a mitten cutter, simply cut out a mitten-shaped
template from card and cut the dough around it using a knife.

60 g/⅓ cup soft dark
    brown sugar
115 g/1 stick butter, softened
1 heaped tablespoon full-fat
    cream cheese
170 g/1¼ cups plain/all-purpose
    flour, sifted, plus extra for
    dusting

FOR THE DECORATION
350 g/1½ cups royal icing/
    confectioners' sugar, sifted
4–5 tablespoons soft shredded
    coconut

mitten-shaped cutter (optional)
large baking sheet, greased and
    lined with baking parchment
piping/pastry bags, fitted with
    a small round nozzle/tip
decorative string/twine

Makes 10

Whisk/beat together the brown sugar and butter until
creamy. Add the cream cheese and flour and mix to a soft
dough. Wrap the dough in clingfilm/plastic wrap and chill
in the fridge for 1 hour.

Preheat the oven to 180°C (350°F) Gas 4.

On a flour-dusted surface, roll out the dough to 5 mm/¼ inch
thick and cut out 10 mitten cookie shapes. Carefully transfer
the cookies to the baking sheet. Bake for 10–12 minutes in
the oven until the cookies turn light golden brown. As soon as
you remove the cookies from the oven, use the icing nozzle/tip
to stamp out a hole in each cookie. Leave the cookies on the
baking sheet for a few minutes, then transfer to a wire rack.

To decorate, place one-third of the icing/confectioners' sugar
in a bowl and mix with a few teaspoons of cold water to make
a stiff, thick icing. Spoon the icing into a piping/pastry bag and
pipe a line as close to the edge of the cookie as possible. Leave
the outline to dry for a few minutes before flooding the cookies
(see page 18) using the remaining icing/confectioners' sugar.
While the icing is still wet, sprinkle the coconut across the
bottom of each to make a fluffy cuff. Leave to set.

Use the remaining stiff icing in the piping/pastry bag to pipe
simple knitted patterns onto each of the mittens. Leave the icing
to set before threading onto string/twine and knotting them
in pairs. The cookies will store for up to 5 days in an airtight
container. It is best to store them flat, in single layers, between
sheets of baking parchment.

Norwegian Butter Cookies

These traditional butter cookies are served at Christmas time in Norway. They are quick to make and taste delicious. If you can't get hold of pearl sugar (also known as nibbed sugar), use flaked/slivered or chopped almonds instead.

300 g/2¼ cups plain/
   all-purpose flour, sifted
1 tablespoon baking powder
a pinch of salt
200 g/1¾ sticks cold butter,
   cut into cubes
125 g/¾ cup plus
   2 tablespoons icing/
   confectioners' sugar
2 teaspoons vanilla sugar
1 egg
1 egg white, lightly beaten,
   for brushing
pearl sugar or chopped
   almonds, for sprinkling

*2–3 baking sheets, lined
   with baking parchment*

Makes about 40

Mix together the flour with the baking powder and a pinch of salt. Add the cubed butter and mix with your fingers until it forms crumbs, then add the icing/confectioners' sugar and vanilla sugar and mix again. Add the whole egg and mix until the dough is even (but don't over-mix).

Put the dough into a bag and leave to chill in the fridge for about 1 hour.

Preheat the oven to 180°C (350°F) Gas 4.

Cut the dough into about 40 equal pieces (about 15 g/½ oz. each), roll them into small balls and place on the lined baking sheets, leaving space between them. Using the back of a fork, press each one down gently in the middle to a diameter of about 3 cm/1¼ inch (they will spread more when baking). If you prefer a flat surface, use the bottom of a glass or similar.

Brush the cookies with the egg white and sprinkle the pearl sugar or chopped almonds over the top.

Bake in the preheated oven for about 10 minutes or until just baked through (don't let them go brown – you want only a slight tinge of colour at the edges). Remove from the oven and leave to cool on wire racks before serving or storing in an airtight container.

Sugar Sprinkle Stars

Sometimes simplicity is best. At Christmas things are often highly decorated and iced and it can be a really indulgent time. These star cookies with citrus bursts taste delicious and are decorated very simply with coloured sugar. The sugar gives a really nice crunchy texture to the cookie and you can use any colours you wish. If you want to use these cookies as tree decorations, simply cut a small hole in them using a large round icing nozzle/tip prior to baking, then thread ribbon through when they are cool. Use a range of different sized cutters, if you wish, to create stacks of twinkling stars that resemble trees, as pictured here.

125 g/9 tablespoons butter, softened
80 g/6½ tablespoons caster/superfine sugar
1 egg
200 g/1½ cups plain/all-purpose flour, plus extra for dusting
grated zest of 1 lemon
1 teaspoon pure vanilla extract or ½ teaspoon vanilla bean powder
coloured crystal sugar

2 large baking sheets, lined with baking parchment
assortment of star-shaped cutters in different sizes

Makes about 24

In a mixing bowl whisk/beat together the butter and sugar until light and creamy. Whisk/beat in the egg. Sift in the flour and mix in well until you have a soft dough, adding the lemon zest and vanilla. Wrap the dough in clingfilm/plastic wrap and chill in the fridge for about 30 minutes.

Preheat the oven to 180°C (350°F) Gas 4.

On a flour-dusted surface, roll out the dough to about 5 mm/¼ inch thick. Cut out star shapes and place on the prepared baking sheets a small distance apart so that they are not touching. Place small stars on one baking sheet and large stars on the other, as the smaller ones will cook more quickly.

Sprinkle each star with a little coloured sugar and bake for 10–15 minutes until the cookies start to turn light golden brown, removing the smaller cookies before the larger cookies to ensure even cooking. Leave to cool on wire racks before serving.

The cookies will store for up to 5 days in an airtight container.

Hot Chocolate Cups
with Candy Cane Handles

These cookies are inspired by one of the nicest things on a cold frosty day – coming home after a walk for a cup of hot chocolate.

FOR THE COOKIES
125 g/9 tablespoons butter, softened
100 g/³/₄ cup icing/confectioners' sugar, sifted
1 egg yolk
180 g/1¹/₄ cups plain/all-purpose flour, sifted, plus extra for dusting
a pinch of salt
a little milk, if needed

FOR THE FILLING
90 g/3¹/₄ oz. dark/bittersweet chocolate
30 g/¹/₄ stick butter
90 ml/¹/₄ cup double/heavy cream

FOR THE DECORATION
200 g/1¹/₂ cups royal icing/confectioners' sugar, sifted
6 candy canes, curved edges cut off for handles
12 mini marshmallows

10-cm/4-inch round cutter
9-cm/3¹/₂-inch flower cutter
6-hole muffin pan, greased
baking beans
piping/pastry bag, fitted with a small round nozzle/tip

Makes 6

Whisk/beat together the butter and icing/confectioners' sugar until light and creamy. Whisk/beat in the egg yolk and mix well. Add the flour and salt, and bring together to a soft dough. If the mixture is too crumbly add a little milk to bind the dough. Wrap in clingfilm/plastic wrap and chill in the fridge for 30 minutes.

Preheat the oven to 180°C (350°F) Gas 4.

On a flour-dusted surface, roll out the dough thinly. Cut out six shapes from each cutter. Place the flower cookies on a baking sheet and bake in the preheated oven for 8–10 minutes until golden brown. Press the six round cookies into the muffin pan holes. Line each cookie with a small square of baking parchment and fill with baking beans. Bake for 10–12 minutes until crisp and golden, and then leave to cool completely in the pan. Once cool, remove the baking beans and paper and, using a teaspoon or sharp knife, carefully lift the cookie cups from the pan.

In a small mixing bowl, mix the royal icing/confectioners' sugar with 2–3 tablespoons water until you have a thick icing. Spoon into the piping/pastry bag and pipe a blob of icing into the centre of each flower cookie. Press a cookie cup on top. Pipe decorative patterns around the rim of the cup. Attach candy cane handles to each cup with a little icing and leave to set.

For the ganache, melt the chocolate, butter and cream in a heatproof bowl set over a pan of simmering water. Whisk/beat together until you have a smooth, thick ganache. Pour into the cups. Decorate with mini marshmallows and leave to set.

These cookies are best eaten on the day they are made, but you can make the cookies 3 days in advance, then fill to serve.

Frosted Pine Cones

Walking through a forest on a crisp winter's morning is a joyful experience, feeling the crunch of twigs and leaves below your feet. I love to collect pine cones which have fallen from the trees and place them in large bowls to decorate the house. These realistic pine cone cookies make a pretty centrepiece for a party table or can be used to decorate a yule log cake. I am not going to lie, adding the almond flakes to each cookie takes time, so this is a job to do accompanied by a few friends and a large glass of mulled wine to keep you all going!

125 g/9 tablespoons butter, softened

80 g/6½ tablespoons caster/superfine sugar

1 egg

180 g/generous ¾ cup plain/all-purpose flour, sifted

50 g/½ cup unsweetened cocoa powder

150 g/scant 1¼ cups marcona or whole blanched almonds

100 g/1¼ cups flaked/slivered almonds

icing/confectioners' sugar, sifted, for dusting

large baking sheet, lined with a silicon mat or baking parchment

Makes 15

Whisk/beat together the butter and sugar until light and creamy. Whisk/beat in the egg, then sift in the flour and cocoa to make a firm dough. Wrap in clingfilm/plastic wrap and chill in the fridge for an hour.

Unwrap the dough and break off small pieces and mould to make 15 cone shapes, each about 5 cm/2 inches high. Place on the prepared baking sheet.

Preheat the oven to 150°C (300°F) Gas 2.

Next you need to make the cone effect using the almonds. First make two rows of whole almonds around the base of each cone, pressing them into the dough so that they are held firm. Make rows of flaked/slivered almonds in rings around each cone, gradually using smaller pieces until you reach the top. Repeat with all the remaining cones.

Bake in the preheated oven for 15–20 minutes . If any of the almonds come out whilst baking, carefully press them in again while the cookie is still warm. Leave to cool on the baking sheet.

Once cool, dust the cookies with a generous dusting of icing/confectioners' sugar to serve.

The cookies will store for up to 3 days in an airtight container.

Ginger Medal Cookies

In Denmark there is a popular afternoon coffee treat known as medaljer, which means 'medals'. They are usually made with shortcrust sweet pastry, but these are a big hit using ginger dough.

½ quantity of Swedish Ginger
  Cookies dough (see page 107)
150 g/1 cup icing/confectioners'
  sugar, plus 1 tablespoon
200 ml/³⁄₄ cup whipping cream
½ teaspoon vanilla sugar or
  pure vanilla extract
½ quantity of Pastry Cream
  (see below)
plain/all-purpose flour,
  for dusting
red berries, to decorate

FOR THE PASTRY CREAM
1 egg yolk
50 g/¼ cup caster/superfine
  sugar
1 tablespoon cornflour/
  cornstarch
250 ml/1 cup whole milk
seeds from ½ vanilla pod/bean
15 g/1 tablespoon butter
a pinch of salt

6–7-cm/2½–2³⁄₄-inch round
  cutter
2 baking sheets, lined
  with baking parchment
2 piping/pastry bags, one fitted
  with a round nozzle/tip
  and one fitted with a star
  nozzle/tip

Makes 6

First, make the pastry cream. In a bowl, whisk/beat together the egg yolk, sugar and cornflour/cornstarch. Place the milk in a pan with the vanilla seeds, bring to the boil, then take the pan off the heat and pour one-third into the egg mixture while whisking/beating. Once whisked, pour back into the pan and bring back to the boil, whisking/beating continuously. Let it thicken for a minute, making sure it does not burn, then remove from the heat and stir in the butter and salt. Pour into a bowl and leave to cool (place baking parchment on top to stop a skin forming). Store in the fridge and use within 2–3 days.

Preheat the oven to 200°C (400°F) Gas 6.

On a flour-dusted surface, roll out the cookie dough to 2 mm/⅛ inch thick. Cut out 16 circles with the cutter (you only need 12, so this allows for extra). Place on the prepared baking sheets and bake in the preheated oven for 6–7 minutes until golden brown. Leave to cool and crisp up on the baking sheet.

Mix the icing/confectioners' sugar with drops of hot water to make a smooth but thick mixture. Put in the piping/pastry bag with the round nozzle/tip and pipe the icing in a neat circle on six of the cookies. Let dry.

Whisk/beat the cream with the vanilla sugar and tablespoon of icing/confectioners' sugar until whipped and stiff, then place in a piping/pastry bag fitted with a star nozzle/tip. Place another six cookies on a plate and spoon 1 tablespoon of pastry cream on each one, then pipe on the whipped cream to a height of 2.5 cm/1 inch. Carefully place the iced cookies on top of the cream. Add more whipped cream and berries to decorate.

Coconut Snowballs

Powdery snow is one of the highlights of winter – perfect for sledging and snowball fights. These are snowball cookies with a crisp coconut cookie base, topped with a gooey coconut meringue and a hidden coconut-chocolate surprise inside.

FOR THE COOKIES
30 g/2½ tablespoons caster/
    superfine sugar
60 g/½ stick butter, softened
90 g/⅔ cup plain/all-purpose
    flour, sifted, plus extra
    for dusting
1 tablespoon cream cheese
60 g/generous ¾ cup soft
    shredded coconut

FOR THE MERINGUE
2 UK large/US extra-large
    egg whites
115 g/generous ½ cup caster/
    superfine sugar
1 teaspoon pure vanilla extract
    or ½ teaspoon vanilla bean
    powder
9 mini coconut chocolates,
    such as Bounty bars or
    Mounds, cut in half
60 g/generous ¾ cup soft
    shredded coconut

5-cm/2-inch round cutter
2 large baking sheets,
    greased and lined with
    baking parchment
ice cream scoop

Makes 18

Begin by making the coconut cookies. In a mixing bowl, whisk/beat together the caster/superfine sugar and butter until soft and creamy. Add the flour and cream cheese and mix to a soft dough. Fold in the coconut. Wrap the dough in clingfilm/plastic wrap and chill in the fridge for 30 minutes.

Preheat the oven to 180°C (350°F) Gas 4.

On a flour-dusted surface, roll out the dough thinly. Cut out 18 rounds of cookie dough using the cutter and place on the prepared baking sheets, leaving space between them. Bake in the preheated oven for about 8–10 minutes until golden brown. Leave to cool on the baking sheets.

Turn the oven temperature down to the lowest setting, about 100°C (200°F) Gas ¼. It is important that the temperature has dropped completely from cooking the cookies before you cook the meringue, otherwise the meringue will turn a caramel colour rather than staying white like a snowball.

In a clean, dry bowl, whisk/beat the egg whites to stiff peaks. Add the sugar a spoonful at a time, whisking/beating all the time. Whisk/beat until all of the sugar is incorporated and you have a smooth, glossy meringue. Whisk/beat in the vanilla.

Place a piece of Bounty or Mounds into the centre of each cookie. Using the ice cream scoop, place scoops of meringue on top of each cookie, making sure the Bounty or Mounds piece is covered. Sprinkle the meringue with the soft shredded coconut. Bake in the preheated oven for about 1–1½ hours until the meringues are crisp but are still white in colour.

The cookies will store for up to 3 days in an airtight container.

Gingerbread Viennese Whirl Sandwich Cookies

I love Viennese whirls – light and crumbly cookies that just melt in the mouth. These are flavoured with gingerbread spices for a festive flavour. If you do not have gingerbread syrup, use ginger syrup instead or any other flavoured syrup of your choosing, such as cinnamon or vanilla.

FOR THE COOKIES
175 g/1½ sticks butter, softened
55 g/generous ⅓ cup icing/
    confectioners' sugar, sifted,
    plus extra for dusting
175 g/1⅓ cups plain/all-purpose
    flour, sifted
60 ml/¼ cup gingerbread syrup
1 teaspoon gingerbread spice
    mix or ground cinnamon

FOR THE FILLING
300 g/2 cups icing/
    confectioners' sugar, sifted
30 g/¼ stick butter, softened
30 g/1 oz. cream cheese
1 tablespoon gingerbread syrup

2 baking sheets, lined
    with baking parchment
2 piping/pastry bags, fitted
    with large star nozzles/tips

Makes 14

Preheat the oven to 180°C (350°F) Gas 4.

In a mixing bowl, cream together the butter and icing/confectioners' sugar. The butter must be very soft, otherwise the dough will be difficult to pipe. Add the flour, syrup and spice, and whisk/beat until you have a smooth, soft dough.

Spoon the dough into one of the piping/pastry bags and pipe 28 rosettes or swirls of the dough onto the prepared baking sheets, leaving space between them.

Bake for 10–12 minutes until golden brown. Watch carefully towards the end of cooking as they can turn dark brown quickly. Leave the cookies to cool on a wire rack. I do this by lifting the baking parchment sheet carefully onto a wire rack.

For the filling, whisk/beat together the icing/confectioners' sugar, butter, cream cheese and syrup until light and creamy. Spoon into the second piping/pastry bag and chill in the fridge until the icing becomes firm.

Bring the icing to room temperature, then pipe a swirl of icing onto the flat side of half of the cookies, then sandwich them together with the un-iced cookies. Place in cake cases to serve and dust with a little icing/confectioners' sugar.

The cookies will store for up to 3 days in an airtight container.

Snowcap Cookies

These cookies have powdered sugar crusts, which resemble snow-capped mountains when the cookies are baked. They are bursting with mouth-watering chocolate, and I don't think anyone would know they are gluten-free!

100 g/3½ oz. plain/semi-sweet
  chocolate, melted and cooled
150 g/1¼ cups gluten-free plain/
  all-purpose flour, sifted
110 g/1 cup ground almonds
2 tablespoons baking powder
a pinch of salt
100 g/½ cup caster/superfine
  sugar
1 egg
100 g/6½ tablespoons butter,
  softened
icing/confectioners' sugar,
  sifted, for dusting

2 baking sheets, greased and
  lined with baking parchment

Makes 18

Place the chocolate, flour, ground almonds, baking powder, salt, caster/superfine sugar, egg and butter in a large mixing bowl, and whisk/beat together to a creamy dough. The dough will seem very soft, but it will become firmer when chilled.

Wrap the dough in baking parchment, and chill in the fridge for 2 hours to set. If you are short of time, you can place the dough in the freezer for 30 minutes, until it is firm.

Preheat the oven to 180°C (350°F) Gas 4.

Divide the dough into 18 pieces, and roll them into small balls between your hands. Roll each ball in icing/confectioners' sugar so they are well coated, then place them on the prepared baking sheet, pressing down slightly with your fingers. Sift over more icing/confectioners' sugar, so that the tops of the cookies are coated in a thick layer of sugar.

Bake for 10–15 minutes until the cookies are just firm. Leave to cool on the baking sheets for a few minutes, then transfer to a wire rack using a spatula.

The cookies will store for up to 3 days in an airtight container.

Clementine Linzer Sandwiches

Linzer cookies are classic Austrian cookies sandwiched with delicious fillings. The cookies in this recipe are flavoured with clementine zest and a pinch of cinnamon for a truly festive feel. I have filled them with clementine curd, but you can use orange or lemon curd if you cannot find a clementine curd. Alternatively, omit the clementine zest and sandwich pairs of cookies around thick salted caramel sauce or dulce de leche for equally delicious results.

140 g/scant ¾ cup caster/
   superfine sugar
125 g/9 tablespoons butter,
   softened
1 egg
250 g/generous 1¾ cups plain/
   all-purpose flour, sifted,
   plus extra for dusting
grated zest of 2 clementines
1 teaspoon ground cinnamon
icing/confectioners' sugar,
   sifted, for dusting
8 tablespoons clementine curd
   (or other citrus fruit curd)

*2 baking sheets, greased and
   lined with baking parchment
linzer cutter or 5-cm/2-inch
   round cutter and small heart
   or flower cutters for the centre*

Makes 24

Preheat the oven to 180°C (350°F) Gas 4.

In a large mixing bowl, whisk/beat together the caster/superfine sugar and softened butter until light and creamy. Add the egg and whisk/beat in. Add the flour, zest and cinnamon and whisk/beat in to form a stiff dough. Wrap in clingfilm/plastic wrap and chill in the fridge for 30 minutes.

On a flour-dusted surface, roll out the dough to about 5 mm/¼ inch thick. Cut out 48 circles with the linzer cutter. Leave 24 cookies whole and cut out centre holes from the other 24 cookies using a small heart or flower cutter.

Transfer to the baking sheets and bake in the preheated oven for 10–12 minutes until crisp and light golden brown. Leave to cool completely on a wire rack.

When cool, dust the cookies that have holes in them with a light coating of icing/confectioners' sugar. It is important to dust with icing/confectioners' sugar before sandwiching the cookies, otherwise the sugar will cover the pretty filling.

Place a teaspoon of curd in the middle of each of the whole cookies and spread out gently. Top with a sugar-dusted cookie (with a hole in).

The cookies will store for up to 3 days in an airtight container, but for the best results, assemble the cookies with the filling just before serving.

Christmas Stars

The decoration on these stars is minimal, but add as much sparkle as you like. Once the icing has dried completely, you could serve the cookies in a towering stack as a table centrepiece.

Gingerbread Cookie Dough
  (see page 14)
plain/all-purpose flour,
  for dusting
Royal Icing (see page 16)
yellow food colouring gel
edible gold glitter
silver sugar stars
edible silver balls

assortment of star-shaped
  cutters
2–3 baking sheets, lined
  with baking parchment
2 piping/pastry bags, fitted
  with small, round nozzles/tips

Makes 10-12

Prepare the gingerbread cookie dough, stopping after you have put the dough in the fridge to chill for at least 1 hour.

Preheat the oven to 170°C (325°F) Gas 3.

Lightly dust a clean work surface with flour and roll the dough evenly to 2–3 mm/⅛ inch thick. Use the cutters to stamp out as many cookies as possible from the dough, cutting each one as close as possible to the next one. Arrange the cookies on the prepared baking sheets and bake the gingerbread in batches on the middle shelf of the preheated oven for 10–12 minutes or until firm and browned at the edges (place smaller stars on one baking sheet and large stars on another, as the smaller ones will cook more quickly). Allow the cookies to cool completely on the baking sheets before icing.

Prepare the royal icing. Transfer about 3 tablespoons to a small bowl and tint yellow using the food colouring. Spoon the yellow icing into a piping/pastry bag and pipe outlines around each cookie. Allow the icing to set for 10 minutes.

Flood the insides of the outlines with the white icing (see page 18). Allow to dry for 5 minutes before scattering edible glitter and sugar stars over the cookies. Pipe small dots of icing onto the point of each star and top with edible silver balls. Allow the icing to dry completely before serving or storing the cookies in an airtight container.

Snowy Peak Cookies

These are very light treats, perfect for when you just need that little hit of sweetness after lunch or dinner. They look like freshly fallen snowy peaks, and they really are as light as snow to eat!

FOR THE COOKIE BASES
300 g/2¼ cups plain/
    all-purpose flour, sifted
2 egg yolks
175 g/1½ sticks butter
2 tablespoons double/heavy
    cream
25 g/1 oz. icing/confectioners'
    sugar, sifted
½ teaspoon grated lemon zest

FOR THE MERINGUE TOPPING
2 egg whites
a tiny pinch of salt
275 g/1½ cups minus
    2 tablespoons caster/
    superfine sugar
1 teaspoon vanilla sugar or
    extract or the seeds from
    1 vanilla pod/bean
1 teaspoon white wine vinegar
3 tablespoons finely chopped
    almonds

baking sheet, greased and
    lined with baking parchment
5-cm/1-inch round fluted cutter
piping/pastry bag, fitted with
    a round nozzle/tip (optional)

Makes 30-35

Blitz the ingredients for the cookie bases briefly in a food processor or blender. Once a smooth cookie dough has formed, wrap in clingfilm/plastic wrap and chill in the fridge for at least 30 minutes.

Preheat the oven to 160°C (300°F) Gas 2.

Roll out the dough on a lightly floured surface to 3 mm/ ⅛ inch thick. Use the cutter to stamp out circles and place them on the prepared baking sheet. Repeat until all the dough has been used.

For the meringue topping, beat the egg whites with a tiny pinch of salt until stiff using a hand-held electric whisk or in a stand mixer with the whisk attachment. Slowly add the sugar and vanilla, bit by bit, and whisk/beat on high speed until you have a shiny mixture that forms stiff peaks (still soft enough to be spoon-able). Fold in the vinegar and chopped almonds.

Pipe or spoon the meringue mixture onto each cookie base, spreading or placing almost to the edge (the meringue will not spread much during baking).

Bake the cookies in the middle of the preheated oven for about 18–20 minutes or until the base is cooked and the top is lightly browned, and the meringue firm but still white. Remove from the oven and leave to cool before serving.

Walnut Cookies

I love to make these pretty walnut praline cookies at Christmas. They look very attractive in the shape of whole walnut shells. To make them you need to invest in a walnut cookie mould, which can be purchased from good cook shops or online stockists (see page 142).

FOR THE WALNUT PRALINE POWDER
100 g/¹/₂ cup caster/superfine sugar
100 g/1 cup walnuts

FOR THE COOKIES
50 g/3 tablespoons butter, chilled
190 g/1¹/₂ cups gluten-free plain/all-purpose flour, sifted
2 tablespoons mascarpone cheese
1 teaspoon ground cinnamon
1 tablespoon caster/superfine sugar
icing/confectioners' sugar, sifted, for dusting

FOR THE FILLING
50 g/3 tablespoons butter, softened
200 ml/generous ³/₄ cup double/heavy cream

silicon mat or baking sheet, greased
walnut-shaped cookie moulds, greased

Makes 18

Begin by preparing the walnut praline powder. Place the caster/superfine sugar in a saucepan and melt over a gentle heat, swirling the pan to ensure that the sugar does not burn. Cook until the caramel starts to turn a light golden brown colour and all the sugar has melted. Spread the walnuts out on the silicon mat or greased baking sheet, and pour over the caramel. Leave to cool completely, then blitz to very fine crumbs in a food processor or blender to make the praline powder.

Preheat the oven to 180°C (350°F) Gas 4.

In a large mixing bowl, rub the butter into the flour until the mixture resembles fine breadcrumbs. Add the mascarpone cheese, cinnamon, sugar and 1 tablespoon of the walnut praline powder, and bring the mixture together to a soft dough with your hands, adding a little cold water if the mixture is too dry.

Press small pieces of the dough into each walnut mould, just filling each hole. Bake in the preheated oven for 10–15 minutes, until the cookies are lightly golden. Leave to cool in the mould for a few minutes, then turn the cookies out onto a wire rack. Clean and re-grease the moulds, then repeat with the remaining dough until you have 36 walnut cookie halves.

For the filling, place the butter, remaining praline powder and double/heavy cream in a bowl and whisk/beat to a stiff mixture.

Place a spoonful of the filling on the flat side of one of the cookies, and sandwich together with another cookie. Repeat with the remaining cookie halves. Serve dusted with icing/confectioners' sugar. The unfilled cookies can be stored for up to 2 days in an airtight container.

Red Velvet Snowcaps

Snowcaps are cookies that have a decorative surface made by dusting them liberally with icing/confectioners' sugar to create a crackled effect on top when they bake. They are said to be inspired by snow-topped mountains. Traditionally chocolate (see page 40), these are my red velvet version.

100 g/3½ oz. dark/bittersweet chocolate, melted and cooled
250 g/generous 1¾ cups plain/all-purpose flour, sifted
2 teaspoons baking powder
a pinch of salt
1 teaspoon pure vanilla extract or ½ teaspoon vanilla bean powder
100 g/½ cup caster/superfine sugar
1 egg, beaten
115 g/1 stick butter, softened
2 teaspoons red food colouring gel
icing/confectioners' sugar, sifted, for dusting

2 baking sheets, greased and lined with baking parchment

Makes 30

Add all the ingredients (excluding the icing/confectioners' sugar) into a bowl and whisk/beat together to a soft dough. Use enough red food colouring gel to make a vibrant red colour. You should be able to mould the dough into balls in your hands without it being too sticky, but if it is too soft, either chill it in the fridge or dust with a little extra flour as you work.

Preheat the oven to 180°C (350°F) Gas 4.

Roll the dough into 30 balls about the size of large walnuts. Roll each ball in icing/confectioners' sugar. Place a small distance apart on the baking sheets and sift again with a generous layer of icing/confectioners' sugar. It is important for there to be plenty of icing/confectioners' sugar as this is what makes the pretty decoration on top of the cookies when they crack open.

Bake in the preheated oven for 10–15 minutes until the tops have cracked. Remove from the oven and leave to cool on a wire rack.

The cookies will store for up to 5 days in an airtight container.

Nordic Spiced Cookies

550 g/4 cups plain/all-purpose
  flour, sifted, plus extra for
  dusting
1 teaspoon bicarbonate of/
  baking soda
1 teaspoon each of ground ginger,
  cloves and cardamom
2 teaspoons ground cinnamon
a pinch of ground allspice
a pinch of salt
150 g/1 stick plus
  2 tablespoons butter, softened
200 g/²/₃ cup golden/light corn
  syrup
100 g/¹/₂ cup granulated sugar
100 g/¹/₂ cup dark brown sugar
150 ml/²/₃ cup double/heavy cream
¹/₂ teaspoon grated orange zest
icing/confectioners' sugar, for
  dusting

2–3 baking sheets, lined
  with baking parchment
assortment of festive-shaped
  cutters

Makes 50–70

These cookies are so simple to make and combine spices most resonant with the festive season, which will make your home smell wonderful and ready for any gathering. Serve them with any kind of warming drink – hot chocolate for the younger members of the group, and maybe something a bit stronger for the adults!

Mix the flour and bicarbonate of/baking soda with all the ground spices and salt. Add the butter and all the other ingredients and mix until you have an even dough. It may still be sticky, but shape into a log and wrap in clingfilm/plastic wrap and leave to chill in the fridge overnight.

Preheat the oven to 200°C (400°F) Gas 6.

On the flour-dusted surface, roll out the dough thinly and use the cutters to cut your desired shapes. You want the cookies to be thin.

Bake in the preheated oven on lined baking sheets – each batch will take 5–6 minutes depending on the thickness. You want the cookies to be a darker shade of brown.

Remove from the oven and cool on a wire rack.

Dust with icing/confectioners' sugar to serve or store in an airtight container.

Almond Crescents

These little nutty cookies look like silvery moons with their dusting of icing/confectioners' sugar. This recipe uses almonds, but you could use chopped mixed nuts instead – simply grind them in the food processor before adding to the mixture. Look out for the bags of ready-chopped mixed nuts in the baking section of the supermarket.

100 g/²/₃ cups icing/
   confectioners' sugar, sifted,
   plus extra for dusting
200 g/1³/₄ stick butter, softened
1 egg yolk
1 teaspoon pure vanilla extract
300 g/2¹/₄ cups plain/
   all-purpose flour, sifted
1 teaspoon baking powder
100 g/1 cup ground almonds,
   hazelnuts or mixed nuts

2 baking sheets, lined
   with baking parchment

Makes about 24

Put the icing/confectioners' sugar, butter, egg yolk and vanilla extract in the bowl of an electric mixer (or use a large bowl and a hand-held electric whisk) and cream the ingredients until smooth and light.

Add the flour, baking powder and ground nuts and mix until the dough comes together into a ball. Flatten into a disc, cover with clingfilm/plastic wrap and chill in the fridge for 1 hour.

Preheat the oven to 180°C (350°F) Gas 4.

Break off a walnut-sized piece of the cookie dough and roll into a short, fat sausage shape in your hands. Bend into a crescent and place on one of the prepared baking sheets. Repeat with the remaining dough, leaving space between them.

Put the sheets on the middle shelf of the preheated oven and bake for about 12 minutes or until golden.

Remove the sheets from the oven. Leave to cool for 2 minutes, then dust with plenty of icing/confectioners' sugar. Leave to cool before serving or storing in an airtight container.

Toffee Cookie Slices

These toffee cookies are super-quick to make. The addition of sea salt flakes to the top gives them a savoury hit, as well as looking like freshly fallen snow. Substitute two tablespoons of the flour with unsweetened cocoa powder to make them chocolate, and experiment with pearl sugar or chopped almonds to create the 'snow'.

140 g/1¼ sticks butter
120 g/generous ½ cup caster/
    superfine sugar
4 tablespoons golden/light
    corn syrup
1½ teaspoons vanilla sugar
1 teaspoon baking powder
300 g/2¼ cups plain/
    all-purpose flour, sifted
½ teaspoon sea salt (optional)

*3 baking sheets, greased and
    lined with baking parchment*

Makes about 36

Preheat the oven to 180°C (350°F) Gas 4.

In a mixing bowl, cream the butter and caster/superfine sugar until pale and fluffy, then add the syrup, followed by the vanilla sugar, baking powder and flour. Mix with your hands until you have an even dough.

Cut the dough into 3 equal pieces. Roll each piece out directly on the prepared baking sheets to the size of 6 x 35 cm/2½ x 14 inches. Sprinkle the salt over the top of the dough, if using.

Bake in the preheated oven for 8–10 minutes. As soon as you remove the biscuits/cookies from oven, use a pizza wheel or sharp knife to cut each rectangle into 12 pieces. Leave to cool on a wire rack before serving.

The cookies will store for up to a week in an airtight container.

Festive Friends

Snowmen Faces

'Do you want to build a snowman?' So the popular movie song goes...
Well, if you do, then why not make these friendly snowy faces! The
cookies are made with marzipan and cocoa and taste scrumptious.

200 g/7 oz. natural marzipan,
    broken into small pieces
90 g/³⁄₄ stick butter, softened
100 g/1 cup ground almonds
100 g/³⁄₄ cup self-raising/
    self-rising flour, sifted,
    plus extra for dusting
40 g/scant ¹⁄₂ cup unsweetened
    cocoa powder
350 g/2¹⁄₂ cups fondant
icing/confectioners' sugar, sifted
orange and black food colouring
    gels

7-cm/2³⁄₄-inch round cutter
2 baking sheets, lined
    with baking parchment
piping/pastry bag, fitted with
    a small round nozzle/tip
cocktails sticks/toothpicks

Makes 20

Preheat the oven to 180°C (350°F) Gas 4.

Cream together the marzipan and butter using a hand-held
electric whisk or stand mixer until it becomes paste-like. Add
the almonds, flour and cocoa, and beat to a smooth dough. It
should be soft but not sticky, so add a little more flour if needed.

On a flour-dusted surface, roll out the dough to 5 mm/¹⁄₄ inch
thick and cut out 20 circles, re-rolling the dough as necessary.
Place the cookies on the baking sheet, leaving space between
them. Bake in the preheated oven for 10–15 minutes. Remove
from the oven and leave to cool on the baking sheets for a few
minutes, then transfer to a wire rack to cool completely.

To ice the cookies mix 300 g/2 cups of the icing/confectioners'
sugar with about 2 tablespoons of water until you have a thick
icing. Spoon one-third into the piping/pastry bag and pipe a
circle around the edge of each cookie. Leave to set for 10 minutes.
Return any icing to the bowl and add a little more water so that
the icing is thin enough to flow. Flood the circles with a spoonful
of icing (see page 18) and leave to set.

Mix the remaining 50 g/¹⁄₂ cup icing/confectioners' sugar
with a little water and mix in a few drops of orange food
colouring. Using a cocktail stick/toothpick, place a line of orange
icing in the centre of each cookie to make a carrot nose. When
you have completed all the noses, add a few drops of black food
colouring to the orange icing, to make it completely black. Using
a second cocktail stick/toothpick, place dots of black icing onto
the cookies for the eyes and mouth. Leave to set.

The cookies will store for up to 5 days in an airtight container.

Santa Cookies

These festive Santas are decorated using royal icing. Simple diamond-shaped cookies give the perfect shape for Santa's hat and beard.

FOR THE COOKIES
115 g/1 stick butter, softened
60 g/5 tablespoons caster/
  superfine sugar
170 g/1¼ cups plain/all-purpose
  flour, sifted, plus extra
  for dusting
grated zest of 2 clementines
a little milk, if needed

FOR THE DECORATION
400 g/scant 3 cups royal icing/
  confectioners' sugar, sifted
red and black food colouring
  gels
large white snowflake sprinkles,
  or similar

*2 baking sheets, greased and
  lined with baking parchment*
*2 piping/pastry bags, fitted with
  small round nozzles/tips*
cocktail sticks/toothpicks

Makes 10

Whisk/beat together the butter and sugar. Add the flour and the zest, and whisk/beat until a soft dough forms, adding milk if needed. Wrap in clingfilm/plastic wrap. Chill in the fridge for 30 minutes.

Preheat the oven to 180°C (350°F) Gas 4.

On a flour-dusted surface, roll the dough to 5 mm/¼ inch thick. Cut out 10 diamonds with 8 cm/3¼ inch sides, re-rolling as necessary. Place on the baking sheets and bake in the preheated oven for 10–15 minutes until the cookies are lightly golden brown. Transfer to a wire rack to cool.

Whisk/beat the icing/confectioners' sugar with 3 tablespoons of water until you have a stiff icing. Colour one-third of the icing red and spoon 2 spoonfuls into a piping/pastry bag. Spoon 5 large spoonfuls of white icing into another. Pipe a fine red line along the top two edges of the cookies. Pipe the outline of the band of Santa's hat with the white, then pipe a half-egg shape below, to outline Santa's face. Scrape the red icing back into its bowl and about half of the white icing back into its bowl. Add a little water to both so that they are thin enough to flow. Spoon a little white icing into a bowl and add red colouring to create a pale pink. Flood pink in the half-egg shapes (see page 18). Do the same with the red icing in the hat outline, and the white icing in the hat's band outline. Dip a cocktail stick/toothpick into the red icing and add rosy cheeks. Add some black food colouring to the pink icing and use a cocktail stick/toothpick to add eyes. Pipe a white curly beard at the base. Pipe a small blob of icing to the top of each hat and affix a sprinkle. Allow to set for 15 minutes.

The cookies will store for up to 5 days in an airtight container.

Reindeer Cookies

320 g/scant 2½ cups self-
raising/self-rising flour
30 g/⅓ cup unsweetened
cocoa powder
1 teaspoon bicarbonate of/
baking soda
200 g/1 cup caster/superfine
sugar
175 g/1½ sticks butter
3 heaped tablespoons
golden/light corn syrup
36 pretzels
17 sugar-coated chocolate
peanuts plus 1 red one
for Rudolf
30 g/1 oz. white chocolate,
broken into pieces
30 g/1 oz. dark/bittersweet
chocolate, broken into pieces

*3 baking sheets, greased and
lined with baking parchment*
*2 piping/pastry bags, fitted with
small round nozzles/tips*

Makes 18

These little reindeer would make any Christmas party a jolly event – they have pretzel antlers and chocolate peanut noses – perfect for guiding Santa on his way! You can use any type of pretzel or chocolate peanut nose, and just give one a red nose for the hero Rudolf!

Preheat the oven to 180°C (350°F) Gas 4.

Sift the flour, cocoa powder and bicarbonate of/baking soda into a bowl. Stir in the sugar. In a saucepan, heat the butter and syrup until the butter has melted. Stir the syrup mixture into the flour and whisk/beat in until the dough comes together.

Divide the dough into 18 pieces and place them in small mounds on the baking sheets, leaving space between them. Press each cookie down to flatten them.

Bake in the preheated oven for 5 minutes, then remove from the oven and press two pretzels into each cookie for the antlers. Using a clean cloth press each cookie down. Return to the oven and bake for a further 5–7 minutes. Remove from the oven and immediately press one sugar-coated chocolate peanut into each cookie for the nose. Leave the cookies to cool on the baking sheets for 5 minutes, then, using a spatula, transfer them to a wire rack to cool completely.

Place the white and dark/bittersweet chocolate into two separate heatproof bowls and rest each bowl over a pan of simmering water. Heat until the chocolate has melted. Leave to cool slightly, then spoon into the piping/pastry bags.

Pipe two small circles of white chocolate onto each cookie as eyes and then pipe a smaller dot of dark chocolate onto the white chocolate for the pupils. Leave to cool completely until the chocolate has set.

The cookies will store for up to 5 days in an airtight container.

Santa Claus Gingerbread

These cute Santa cookies have been made using an extra-large, simple gingerbread man cutter. The icing is slightly more fiddly, but the recipe only makes about 6 cookies, so it's quite doable and looks beautiful!

**Gingerbread Cookie Dough
(see page 14)**
**plain/all-purpose flour,
for dusting**
Royal Icing (see page 16)
**red and black food colouring
gels**
white sugar sprinkles

*20-cm/8-inch-tall
gingerbread man cutter*
*2–3 baking sheets, lined
with baking parchment*
*3 piping/pastry bags, fitted
with small round nozzles/tips*

Makes about 6

Prepare the gingerbread cookie dough, stopping after you have put the dough in the fridge to chill for at least 1 hour.

Preheat the oven to 170°C (325°F) Gas 3.

On a flour-dusted surface, roll out the dough to an even thickness. Cut out the cookies, re-rolling as necessary. Arrange the cookies on the baking sheets, leaving space between them. Bake in batches on the middle shelf of the preheated oven for 10–12 minutes or until firm and lightly browned. Remove from the oven and leave to cool completely on the baking sheets.

Prepare the royal icing. Spoon three quarters of the icing into a bowl and tint it red using the food colouring. Tint a further 3 tablespoons black in a small bowl. Leave the remaining icing white. Fill a piping/pastry bag with 2 tablespoons of the red icing and pipe an outline around the bottom half of each man in the shape of a pair of trousers. Do the same in a jacket shape around the top half. Pipe an outline for a hat. Fill another piping/pastry bag with the black icing and pipe an outline for the boots. Fill another piping/pastry bag with the white icing and pipe outlines for the fur trim on the hat, collar, belt, and sleeve and trouser cuffs. Allow to dry for at least 10 minutes then flood each section (see page 18) with the corresponding colours. Scatter the white sugar sprinkles over the white areas and allow to dry for 20 minutes.

Finally, pipe white buttons down the middle of Santa's jacket, a black buckle on his belt and 2 eyes and a big red nose. Leave to set completely before serving.

Carrots for Rudolf

FOR THE COOKIES
60 g/5 tablespoons caster/
    superfine sugar
115 g/1 stick butter, softened
170 g/1¼ cups plain/all-purpose
    flour, sifted, plus extra
    for dusting
1 tablespoon milk

FOR THE DECORATION
200 g/7 oz. white chocolate
orange and green food
    colouring gels

carrot-shaped cutter
large baking sheet, greased and
    lined with baking parchment
2 piping/pastry bags, fitted with
    small round nozzles/tips

Makes 16

My niece and nephew who live in America enjoy leaving cookies and milk out for Santa on Christmas Eve. Here in the UK, I leave a sherry and a mince pie! Universal, though, is leaving carrots for his reindeer.

Whisk/beat together the caster/superfine sugar and butter until soft and creamy. Add the flour and milk and mix to a soft dough. Wrap the dough in clingfilm/plastic wrap and chill in the fridge for 30 minutes.

Preheat the oven to 180°C (350°F) Gas 4.

On a flour-dusted surface, roll out the dough to about 5 mm/¼ inch thick and cut out 16 carrot shapes using the cutter. If you do not have a carrot-shaped cutter, cut a template out of cardboard and then cut round the template on the dough using a sharp knife. Place the cookies on the baking sheet and bake in the preheated oven for 10–12 minutes, until lightly golden, but not brown. Leave on the baking sheet to cool for a few minutes, then transfer to a wire rack.

Break the white chocolate into pieces and put it in a heatproof bowl. Rest the bowl over a pan of simmering water until the chocolate is melted, then remove it from the heat and leave it to cool for a few minutes. Colour two-thirds of the white chocolate orange and one-third green.

Place a small amount of each coloured chocolate into a piping/pastry bag. Pipe the outline of the carrot in orange and the outline of the leaves in green. Leave to set before filling the orange carrots with the remaining orange chocolate and filling the green tops with the remaining green chocolate. Leave in a cool place for the chocolate to set before serving.

The cookies will store for up to 3 days in an airtight container.

Jolly Penguins

These fun penguins are great to make with children during the holidays. If penguin-shaped cutters are difficult to find, you can draw penguin shapes on baking parchment and use these as a template or, if you're feeling brave, cut out the shapes freehand. Rolled fondant can easily be moulded into shape, so don't worry about being too accurate.

Gingerbread Cookie Dough
    (see page 14) or Vanilla
    Cookie Dough (see page 15)
icing/confectioners' sugar,
    for dusting
100 g/3½ oz. orange rolled
    fondant (see page 19)
edible glue
250 g/9 oz. black rolled fondant
100 g/3½ oz. white rolled
    fondant
100 g/3½ oz. red rolled fondant

*penguin-shaped cutter
    (optional)*
*baking parchment templates
    (optional)*
cocktail stick/toothpick

Makes 12

Prepare and bake your chosen cookie dough using a penguin-shaped cutter or a baking parchment template.

Dust a clean work surface with icing/confectioners' sugar and roll out the orange rolled fondant. Cut out the feet using your template, if using, and a sharp knife. Attach the orange rolled fondant to the cookies using edible glue, and mark indents on the feet with a cocktail stick/toothpick.

Roll out some black rolled fondant and cut out the penguins' bodies using your template, if using, and a sharp knife. Gently roll over each cookie to attach. Roll out the white rolled fondant and cut out oval shapes using a sharp knife for tummies. Attach them to the cookies. Roll out the red rolled fondant and cut out the hats. Attach a hat to each of the cookies.

To make the eyes, roll 2 small balls of white rolled fondant between your fingers. Squash the middle of the balls to make oval shapes and then squash them flat. Attach them to the cookies and stick 2 tiny balls of black rolled fondant to them for the pupils. To make the beaks, roll a ball of orange rolled fondant between your fingers. Pinch one end of the ball to make it into a triangle shape, then squash it flat. Attach them to the cookies.

To finish the hats, roll a ball of white fondant and attach one to the top of each. Roll a thin sausage of white rolled fondant for the trim of the hats. Attach to the cookies and mark lines along each piece of trim with a cocktail stick/toothpick for texture.

Polar Bear Snow Globes

I have loved snow globes ever since I was a child. There is something magical about watching a glittering snowfall settle on a wintery scene.

FOR THE COOKIES
115 g/1 stick butter, softened
60 g/5 tablespoons caster/
   superfine sugar
1 teaspoon pure vanilla extract
a pinch of salt
170 g/1¼ cups plain/all-purpose
   flour, sifted, plus extra
   for dusting
a little milk, if needed

FOR THE DECORATION
500 g/generous 3½ cups
   royal icing/confectioners'
   sugar, sifted
blue and black food colouring
   gels

polar bear template drawn onto
   baking parchment, each polar
   bear about 4 cm/1¾ inches
   in length
3 piping/pastry bags, one fitted
   with a round nozzle/tip and
   one with a star nozzle/tip
9-cm/3½-inch round cutter
8-cm/3¼-inch round cutter
2 baking sheets, lined with
   baking parchment
cocktail sticks/toothpicks

Makes 6

Mix 100 g/¾ cup of the icing/confectioners' sugar with a few teaspoons of water until you have a stiff icing. Using a round nozzle/tip, pipe the outline of the bear on the template. Leave to dry. Add a little more water to make the icing a little thinner and spoon into the outlines. Add black food colouring to the icing and, using a cocktail stick/toothpick, add an eye and nose. Leave to set.

Cream together the butter and sugar. Add the vanilla, salt and flour and mix to a soft dough. Add a little milk, if needed. Wrap the dough in clingfilm/plastic wrap. Chill in the fridge for 30 minutes.

Preheat the oven to 180°C (350°F) Gas 4.

On a flour-dusted surface, roll out the dough to 5 mm/¼ inch thick. Cut six rounds with the large cutter and place on a baking sheet. Use the small cutter to cut out the centre, leaving a ring. Re-roll the dough and press the large cutter three-quarters of the way into the dough six times. Don't press all the way around as you need to cut out the snow globe base. Using a knife, cut out a curved rectangle along the uncut part of the circle. Place on a baking sheet. Bake in the preheated oven for 10–15 minutes until golden brown. Carefully transfer to a wire rack to cool.

Put the remaining icing/confectioners' sugar in a bowl and add 65 ml/¼ cup of water until you have a smooth, thick icing. Colour half the icing blue and pipe a ring around the edge of the globe cookies and leave to set. Add a little more water to the blue icing so that it flows, and spoon into the six blue rings to fill. Place a polar bear on each globe and use a cocktail stick/toothpick to add dots of the white icing for snow. Place the cookie rings on top. Pipe white icing on the base of the globe using the star nozzle/tip. The cookies will store for up to 5 days in an airtight container.

Coffee Cookies with Vintage Edible Transfers

FOR THE COOKIES
115 g/1 stick butter, softened
200 g/1 cup caster/superfine
    sugar
2½ tablespoons espresso,
    cooled
1 egg
a pinch of salt
1 teaspoon pure vanilla extract
    or ½ teaspoon vanilla bean
    powder
280 g/generous 2 cups self-
    raising/self-rising flour,
    plus extra for dusting

FOR THE ICING
400 g/3 cups royal icing/
    confectioners' sugar, sifted
60–80 ml/¼–⅓ cup espresso,
    cooled
18 edible transfers

*2 baking sheets, greased and
    lined with baking parchment
piping/pastry bag, fitted with
    a small round nozzle/tip
    or a small leaf nozzle/tip*

Makes 18

In this modern age, there are some wonderful products to enhance your baking, such as edible printed icing or rice paper sheets that create stunning effects seen here.

Whisk/beat together the butter and sugar until light and creamy. Add the cooled espresso coffee and whisk/beat in with the egg. Add the salt, vanilla and flour, and whisk/beat until you have a soft dough. Wrap the dough in clingfilm/plastic wrap and chill in the fridge for 30 minutes.

Preheat the oven to 180°C (350°F) Gas 4.

On a flour-dusted surface, roll out the dough to 5 mm/¼ inch thick. Using a sharp knife, cut out 18 rectangles, about 12 x 8 cm/ 5 x 3¼ inches each, re-rolling as necessary. The actual size you need will depend on the size of transfers. The cookies will expand a little during baking, so cut to the size of your transfers, then, when baked, there should be a small border for the icing.

Transfer them to the prepared baking sheets using a spatula and bake in the preheated oven for 10–15 minutes until golden brown. Transfer to a wire rack and leave to cool completely.

For the icing, whisk/beat the icing/confectioners' sugar and coffee together in a bowl (adding the coffee gradually as you may not need it all) until you have a stiff icing. Use a round-bladed knife to spread a thin layer of icing over the top of each cookie and press on a transfer. Spoon the remaining icing into the piping/pastry bag and pipe lines or ruffles of icing around the edge of the pictures. Leave to set.

The cookies will store for up to 5 days in an airtight container.

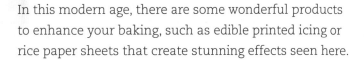

Gingerbread Whoopie Pies

FOR THE WHOOPIE PIES
60 g/⅓ cup sultanas/golden raisins
60 ml/¼ cup gingerbread liqueur
125 g/1 stick butter, softened
200 g/1 cup light brown soft sugar
1 UK large/US extra-large egg
320 g/2½ cups self-raising/self-rising flour
1 teaspoon baking powder
2 teaspoons ground cinnamon
1 teaspoon each ground mixed spice and ground ginger
½ teaspoon salt
250 ml/1 cup sour cream
100 ml/⅓ cup hot water

FOR THE TOPPING
450 g/3⅔ cups royal icing/confectioners' sugar
white edible mimosa balls
mini reindeer and/or Christmas tree decorations

FOR THE FILLING
125 g/1 stick butter
50 ml/3 tablespoons sour cream
350 g/2¾ cups icing/confectioners' sugar
50 ml/3 tablespoons gingerbread syrup

2 x 12-hole whoopie pie pans, greased
piping/pastry bag, fitted with a large star nozzle/tip

Makes 12

These whoopie pies inspired by German gingerbread, lebkuchen, are the perfect treat for festive celebrations. Let your imagination run wild with the snowy scene.

Begin by soaking the sultanas/golden raisins in the gingerbread liqueur for several hours, so that they become plump and juicy.

Preheat the oven to 180°C (350°F) Gas 4.

To make the pies, cream together the butter and brown sugar for 2–3 minutes using an electric hand-held mixer, until light and creamy. Add the egg, sultanas/golden raisins and their soaking liquid and mix again. Sift the flour, baking powder and spices into the bowl, and add the salt and sour cream. Whisk/beat again until everything is incorporated. Add the hot water and whisk/beat into the mixture.

Put a large spoonful of mixture into each hole of the pans. Leave to stand for 10 minutes then bake in the preheated oven for 10–12 minutes. Remove the pies from the oven, leave to cool slightly, then turn out onto a wire rack to cool completely.

To make the icing, whisk/beat the royal icing/confectioners' sugar with 75 ml/⅓ cup cold water for about 5 minutes, until the icing is very stiff. Put a tablespoonful of icing on 12 of the pie halves and use a fork to form it into sharp peaks. Arrange a ring of white edible mimosa balls around the outside edge then add a reindeer or Christmas tree to each pie. Leave to set.

To make the filling, whisk/beat together the butter, sour cream, icing/confectioners' sugar and gingerbread syrup using an electric hand-held mixer, until light and creamy. Spoon the filling into the prepared piping/pastry bag and pipe a swirl onto the un-iced pie halves. Top with the iced pie halves and serve. These are best eaten on the day they are made.

Meringue Snowmen Cookies

These white chocolate chip cookies are flavoured with Lotus Biscoff spread, which gives a delicious spiced caramel flavour. They will keep for a few days, but are best eaten on the day they are made.

FOR THE SNOWMEN
1 egg white
60 g/5 tablespoons caster/
    superfine sugar

FOR THE COOKIES
115 g/1 stick butter, softened
130 g/²/₃ cup caster/superfine
    sugar
60 g/scant ¼ cup full-fat cream
    cheese
60 g/2 oz. Lotus Biscoff spread
    or peanut butter
170 g/1¼ cups self-raising/
    self-rising flour, sifted
100 g/3½ oz. white chocolate
    chips

FOR THE DECORATION
140 g/5 oz. white chocolate,
    melted
3 tablespoons icing/
    confectioners' sugar, sifted
orange and black food colouring
    gels

piping/pastry bag, fitted with
    a large round nozzle/tip
2 large baking sheets, lined
    with baking parchment
cocktail sticks/toothpicks

Makes 14

Preheat the oven to very low, about 130°C (260°F) Gas ½.

Begin by making the snowmen. Whisk/beat the egg white to stiff peaks. Gradually add the sugar, whisking/beating constantly until the meringue is smooth and glossy. Spoon the meringue into the piping/pastry bag and pipe 14 circles about 3 cm/1¼ inch in diameter on one of the baking sheets. On top of each, pipe a smaller ball for the snowman's body, and then a third slightly smaller one on top for the head. Bake in the preheated oven for 45–60 minutes until the meringue is crisp. Leave to cool on the baking sheet.

Increase the oven temperature to 180°C (350°F) Gas 4.

Whisk/beat together the butter, sugar and cream cheese until light and creamy. Add the spread and whisk/beat in. Add the flour and chocolate chips, and whisk/beat in. Put 14 spoonfuls of the dough on the second baking sheet a small distance apart. Bake in the preheated oven for 10–15 minutes until the cookies are lightly golden brown. Leave to cool for a few minutes on the baking sheet and then transfer to a rack to cool completely.

Spoon a little of the melted white chocolate over each of the cookies and place a meringue snowman in the centre of each.

In a mixing bowl, mix the icing/confectioners' sugar with a little water and orange food colouring. Use a cocktail stick/toothpick to draw noses on each of the snowmen. Add a little black food colouring to the icing and then use a second cocktail stick/toothpick to add small black eyes, mouths, buttons and arms. Leave for the icing and white chocolate to set.

The cookies will store for up to 3 days in an airtight container.

Snow Dove Cookies

These simple sugar cookies, cut in the shape of birds in flight, look wintery and magical when sprinkled with a little sugar and some crystal-white edible sparkle. They are very elegant when used as place settings on a festive table, simply tie on a handwritten name card with a fine ribbon as shown.

FOR THE COOKIES
115 g/1 stick butter, softened
50 g/¼ cup caster/superfine
  sugar
1 egg
200 g/1²⁄₃ cups plain/
  all-purpose flour, plus extra
  for dusting
1 tablespoon ground almonds

FOR THE DECORATION
50 g/⅓ icing/confectioners'
  sugar
2 teaspoons freshly squeezed
  lemon juice
granulated sugar and white
  edible sparkle, for sprinkling

*8-cm/3¼-inch dove-shaped
  cutter*
2 baking sheets, greased

Makes about 24

In a large mixing bowl, beat together the butter and sugar until pale and creamy. Beat in the egg, then sift the flour and almonds over the mixture and fold to combine. Knead gently to make a soft dough, then press into a ball, wrap in clingfilm/plastic wrap and chill for about an hour.

Preheat the oven to 180°C (350°F) Gas 4.

Roll out the dough on a lightly floured surface to 4 mm/⅛ inch thick and cut out dove shapes. Place the doves on the prepared baking sheets and bake in the preheated oven for about 10 minutes, until the cookies are a light golden brown. Leave to cool for a couple of minutes on the sheet, then transfer the cookies to a wire rack to cool completely.

To decorate, mix together the icing/confectioners' sugar and lemon juice until smooth. Brush a thin layer of the mixture over a cookie with a pastry brush and sprinkle generously with granulated sugar. Repeat with the remaining cookies. When dry, shake off the excess sugar and sprinkle over a small amount of white edible sparkle.

The cookies will store for up to 4 days in an airtight container.

Deck the Halls

Wreath Cookies

175 g/1½ sticks butter, softened
60 g/scant ½ cup icing/
   confectioners' sugar, sifted
180 g/1⅓ cups plain/all-purpose
   flour, sifted
1 teaspoon pure vanilla extract
   or ½ teaspoon vanilla bean
   powder
red sugar sprinkles (optional)

*piping/pastry bag, fitted
   with a star nozzle/tip
2 baking sheets, greased and
   lined with baking parchment*

Makes 12

Hanging a wreath on a front door is the beginning of Christmas for me – it is a sign to everyone passing my home that the festivities have started inside. These pretty wreath-inspired cookies are made with a buttery Viennese dough sweetened with icing/confectioners' sugar. These are made with vanilla but you can vary the flavour by adding citrus zest or peppermint extract, if you prefer.

In a mixing bowl, whisk/beat together the butter and icing/confectioners' sugar until light and creamy. Sift in the flour and add the vanilla, then whisk/beat together to make a soft dough.

Spoon the dough into the piping/pastry bag and pipe 12 rings of stars in wreath shapes onto the lined baking sheets. Sprinkle over the red sugar sprinkles, if using. Chill in the freezer for 30 minutes until firm.

Preheat the oven to 180°C (350°F) Gas 4.

Bake the cookies in the preheated oven for about 10 minutes until the cookies are just firm. Take care towards the end of cooking as the cookies can turn slightly brown, so you need to remove them before they start to discolour. Leave to cool completely on the baking sheets before looping a ribbon through each one for decoration.

The cookies will store for up to 5 days in an airtight container.

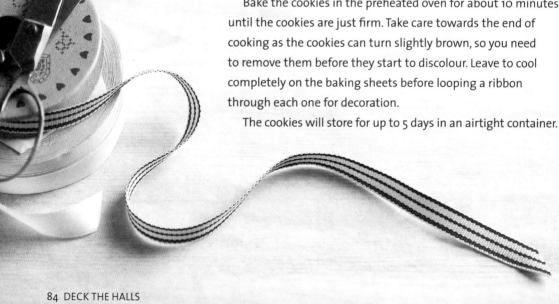

Christmas Pudding Cookies

Making Christmas puddings is one of my family's traditions –
every year on 'Stir Up Sunday' we make our puddings to my great
grandmother's recipe – all taking turns to stir and make a wish.
I love the rich flavours of the boozy fruit, oranges and spices. These
cookies, made using crumbled Christmas pudding (or fruit cake) and
decorated with white chocolate and sugar holly, look truly festive!

FOR THE COOKIES
350 g/2²/₃ cups self-raising/
   self-rising flour
1 teaspoon bicarbonate of/
   baking soda
200 g/1 cup caster/superfine
   sugar
grated zest of 1 large orange
2 teaspoons ground cinnamon
175 g/1½ sticks butter
3 heaped tablespoons golden/
   light corn syrup
100 g/3½ oz. leftover cooked
   Christmas pudding or dense,
   crumbly fruit cake

FOR THE DECORATION
150 g/5 oz. white chocolate,
   broken into pieces
18 sugar holly decorations

*2 baking sheets, greased and
   lined with baking parchment*

Makes 18

Preheat the oven to 180°C (350°F) Gas 4.

Sift the flour and bicarbonate of/baking soda into a mixing
bowl. Stir in the sugar, orange zest and ground cinnamon. In a
saucepan, heat the butter and syrup until the butter has melted.
Break the Christmas pudding (or cake) into small pieces and stir
into the warm syrup mixture. It will soften and dissolve slightly.
Stir the syrup mixture into the flour and whisk/beat in until
you have a crumbly dough. Bring the dough together with
your hands.

Divide the dough into 18 pieces and place in small mounds on
the baking sheets, leaving space between them. Press the dough
down with your fingertips. Bake in the preheated oven for about
10–12 minutes, then remove from the oven. Leave the cookies
to cool on the baking sheets for 5 minutes, as they will be soft
when you remove them from the oven, then use a spatula to
transfer them to a wire rack to cool completely.

Melt the white chocolate in a heatproof bowl resting over a
pan of simmering water, then leave to cool slightly. Spoon the
chocolate over the top third of each cookie in a drizzled pattern
that resembles a Christmas pudding. Top each cookie with a
sugar holly decoration and leave until the chocolate has set.

The cookies will store for up to 5 days in an airtight container.

Treacle House Cookies

Have fun adorning these little houses, using different sweets/candies for decoration. Use a variety of house-shaped cutters to create a whole snow-covered gingerbread village. The number of cookies you make will depend on the size of the cutters you use.

FOR THE COOKIES
2 heaped tablespoons
   black treacle/molasses
70 g/²/₃ stick butter
200 g/1¹/₂ cups plain/all-purpose
   flour, sifted
1 teaspoon bicarbonate of/
   baking soda
2 teaspoons ground cinnamon
1 egg
85 g/7 tablespoons caster/
   superfine sugar

FOR THE ICING
450 g/3¹/₄ cups icing/
   confectioners' sugar, sifted
2 egg whites
1 teaspoon glycerine
1 tablespoon freshly squeezed
   lemon juice
candies and/or edible sparkles,
   to decorate (optional)

assortment of house, tree,
   snowflake and star cutters
2 large baking sheets, greased
   and lined with baking
   parchment
piping/pastry bag, fitted
   with a round nozzle/tip

Makes about 15

Heat the treacle/molasses and butter in a pan and leave to cool. Place the cooled butter mixture in a mixing bowl with the flour, bicarbonate of/baking soda, cinnamon, egg and sugar, and whisk/beat together. Leave the dough to rest for an hour or so, until it is firm enough to roll out.

Preheat the oven to 180°C (350°F) Gas 4.

On a flour-dusted surface, roll out the dough to about 5 mm/¹/₄ inch thick. If the dough is still very soft, add a little more flour. Cut out house shapes, trees, stars and snowflakes until all the dough is used up, re-rolling as necessary. (Try not to re-roll the dough too much though, as it will become crumbly and dry.) Using a spatula, put the gingerbread onto the baking sheets and bake in the preheated oven for 10–12 minutes until firm to the touch. Leave to cool slightly on the sheets, then carefully cut out doors and windows using a sharp knife.

For the icing, whisk/beat together the icing/confectioners' sugar, egg whites, glycerine and lemon juice until the icing is light and holds a peak. Add a little more lemon juice if the mixture is too stiff. It is important to whisk/beat the icing for about 3 minutes to beat in as much air as possible.

Spoon the icing into the piping/pastry bag and pipe 'snow' onto the houses. With the icing, stick gingerbread snowflakes and/or stars onto the roof. Whilst the icing is still soft, add candies or edible white sparkle, if you like. Leave the icing to set before serving or arranging as a decoration.

The cookies will store for up to 5 days in an airtight container.

Frosted Snowflakes

These pretty snowflakes are perfect for decorating the house, for giving as gifts and for eating and enjoying. Not only do they taste great, but they look stunning hung from silvery, decorated branches or on the Christmas tree.

Gingerbread Cookie Dough
(see page 14)
plain/all-purpose flour,
for dusting
icing/confectioners' sugar,
for dusting
250 g/8 oz. ready-to-roll icing
2 tablespoons apricot jam/jelly,
warmed
4 tablespoons Royal Icing
(see page 16)
edible silver balls

*assortment of
snowflake-shaped cutters
2–3 baking sheets, lined
with baking parchment
piping/pastry bag fitted with
a small round nozzle/tip
tiny star-shaped embossing tools*

Makes 10-12

Prepare the gingerbread cookie dough, stopping after you have put the dough in the fridge to chill for at least 1 hour.

Preheat the oven to 170°C (325°F) Gas 3.

Lightly dust a clean work surface with flour and roll out the dough to an even thickness. Cut out as many cookies as possible from the dough, re-rolling as necessary. Arrange the cookies on the prepared baking sheets, leaving space between them. Bake the gingerbread in batches on the middle shelf of the preheated oven for 10–12 minutes or until firm and lightly browned at the edges. Leave the cookies to cool completely on the baking sheets before icing.

Lightly dust the work surface with icing/confectioners' sugar and roll out the ready-to-roll icing to a thickness of no more than 2 mm/1⁄16 inch. Using the same snowflake cutters as above, stamp out shapes from the icing to match your cookies. Brush apricot jam/jelly lightly over each cookie and carefully position the icing snowflakes on top. Gently press the icing snowflakes in place.

Prepare just 4 tablespoons of the royal icing. Fill the piping bag with the royal icing and pipe delicate lines across some of the snowflakes. Use the embossing tool to press delicate patterns into the fondant icing. Stick edible silver balls to the snowflakes with a dot of royal icing. Allow the royal icing to set completely before threading the cookies with fine ribbon.

Candy Cane Cookies

Baked almond marzipan is one of my favourite things and here it makes delicious candy canes. The dough takes food colouring really well, which allows you to make beautifully striped candy canes, just with the dough itself, without the need for icing.

200 g/7 oz. natural marzipan, broken into small pieces
90 g/³/₄ stick butter, softened
100 g/1 cup ground almonds
100 g/scant ½ cup self-raising/ self-rising flour, sifted, plus extra for dusting
1 teaspoon pure vanilla extract
red food colouring gel

2 large baking sheets, greased and lined with baking parchment

Makes about 18

Preheat the oven to 150°C (300°F) Gas 2.

Cream together the marzipan and butter using a hand-held electric whisk (or in a stand mixer) until the mixture becomes paste-like. Add the ground almonds, flour and vanilla and whisk/beat to a smooth, soft dough. The mixture should be soft but not sticky, so add a little more flour if needed.

Divide the mixture into two and add a little red food colouring gel to one half, mixing it in so that it is an even colour.

On a flour-dusted surface, take a small piece of the uncoloured dough and roll it out into a long sausage shape. Repeat with a same-sized piece of the red dough and roll out to the same size as the first one. Press the two sausage shapes together to bind the dough and then twist gently, so that it alternates in a red and white pattern. Use your fingertips to roll the dough together so that it is smooth, then transfer to one of the baking sheets and bend into a candy cane shape. Repeat with all the remaining dough.

Bake the cookies in the preheated oven for 15–20 minutes until the uncoloured dough just starts to turn a light golden colour. It is important to cook the cookies on a low heat as in a hot oven the dough will brown too much and you will lose the red and white coloured effect. Remove from the oven and leave to cool on the baking sheets.

The cookies will store for up to 5 days in an airtight container.

Snow Scene Cookies

Shortbread dough can be coloured, creating pretty edible treats. These starry scenes make a great gift, in cellophane bags tied with ribbon.

60 g/5 tablespoons caster/
   superfine sugar
115 g/1 stick butter, softened
170 g/1¼ cups plain/all-purpose
   flour, sifted, plus extra
   for dusting
1 tablespoon milk, if needed
blue and green food colouring
   gels
30 g/1 oz. white chocolate,
   broken into pieces
gold sugar star sprinkles
icing/confectioners' sugar,
   for dusting

*baking sheet, greased and
   lined with baking parchment*
miniature tree-shaped cutter

Makes 12

Whisk/beat together the sugar and butter until light and creamy. Add the flour and whisk/beat in until the mixture comes together in a soft dough (adding a little milk if it is dry).

Divide the dough in two. Colour one piece with blue food colouring and roll it into a sausage shape, about 15 cm/6 inches long. Mould two-thirds of the uncoloured dough into a semi-circle shape the same length as the blue dough. Press the two doughs together and roll on a flour-dusted surface so that the two come together and you have a sausage shape that is mainly blue with a white part at the bottom. Wrap in clingfilm/plastic wrap. Colour the remaining dough green and wrap in clingfilm/plastic wrap. Chill all the dough in the fridge for an hour.

Preheat the oven to 180°C (350°F) Gas 4.

Using a sharp knife, slice the cylinder of blue and white dough into 12 equal rounds and arrange on a baking sheet.

On a flour-dusted surface, roll out the green dough very thinly. Using the cutter, cut out small green trees and place on the rounds of cookie dough, pressing them down so that the base of the trees are in the white 'snow' and the tops are in the blue 'sky'. Bake in the preheated oven for 10–12 minutes, then remove from the oven and leave to cool on a wire rack.

Melt the white chocolate in a heatproof bowl resting over a pan of simmering water. Leave to cool for a few minutes, then using a cocktail stick/toothpick, put small dots of chocolate in the 'sky' and press on the sugar star sprinkles. Leave the cookies somewhere cool for the chocolate to set. Dust with icing/confectioners' sugar before serving.

The cookies will store for up to 5 days in an airtight container.

Snowflake Cookies

The true beauty of snowflakes is that each one of the tiny icy shapes is unique. When you look at them closely they are spectacularly pretty and intricate. This light cream cheese-enriched cookie dough can be piped into pretty shapes, so let your creativity shine. You can use different nozzles/tips to create different patterns, if you like.

125 g/9 tablespoons butter,
    softened
100 g/½ cup caster/superfine
    sugar
60 g/scant ¼ cup full-fat
    cream cheese
1 egg
170 g/1¼ cups plain/all-purpose
    flour, sifted, plus extra
    for dusting
icing/confectioners' sugar,
    for dusting

piping/pastry bag, fitted with
    a small round nozzle/tip
2 baking sheets, lined with
    baking parchment

Makes 15

Preheat the oven to 180°C (350°F) Gas 4.

Cream together the butter and caster/superfine sugar until light and creamy. Add the cream cheese and whisk/beat in, then add the egg and whisk/beat a little more. Sift in the flour and whisk/beat until you have a very soft dough.

Spoon the dough into the piping/pastry bag and pipe snowflakes in different patterns onto the baking sheets. It is important that, although different shapes, the cookies are of a similar size so that they cook evenly. If you want to make some small and some large, use different baking sheets for each size so that you can take each baking sheet out of the oven when its batch of cookies is cooked.

Bake in the preheated oven for 8–12 minutes until the cookies are firm and lightly golden, but not brown. Remove from the oven and leave to cool on the baking sheets.

Dust the cooled cookies with a thick layer of icing/confectioners' sugar to make them white like snowflakes. The cookies should be lifted very carefully, as they will be fragile given the thin lines of each snowflake.

The cookies will keep for up to 3 days in an airtight container.

Baubles

These bauble cookies make lovely Christmas tree decorations.
Go for turquoise, red and white for a vintage look or opt for
richer colours, such as purples or reds, for a traditional festive
look. Making these cookies from gingerbread makes your
house smell wonderfully festive, but vanilla works well too.

**Gingerbread Cookie Dough
  (see page 14) or Vanilla
  Cookie Dough (see page 15)**
**½ recipe each white, turquoise
  and red Royal Icing (page 16)**
edible glitter

*assortment of bauble-shaped
  cutters*
*3 piping/pastry bags, fitted
  with fine round nozzles/tips*
ribbon

Makes 12

Prepare and bake your chosen cookie dough
using an assortment of bauble-shaped cutters,
making a small hole with the nozzle/tip of a
piping/pastry bag in the top of each cookie
before baking.

Outline and flood them (see page 18)
with royal icing in colours of your choice.

Pipe simple patterns onto the cookies
in different colours to decorate, using the
remaining coloured royal icing left over from
outlining the cookies.

While the cookies are still wet, sprinkle with
edible glitter. To get a light, even covering, put
some glitter on the end of a spatula or table
knife and gently tap the side of the knife while
holding it over the cookies.

Finally, thread ribbon through the cookies
so that they can be hung up.

Garland Cookies

These pretty little cardamom-spiced cookies are threaded together to make a delicate garland to adorn your Christmas dining table, festive buffet or cookie swap display. If you want to give them as a gift, present them in a labelled glass clip-top preserving jar along with a pretty length of string/twine.

160 g/scant 1¼ cup plain/
   all-purpose flour, sifted,
   plus extra for dusting
50 g/½ cup ground almonds
½ teaspoon baking powder
50 g/¼ cup caster/superfine
   sugar
a pinch of salt
100 g/7 tablespoons butter,
   softened
1 egg yolk
½ teaspoon ground cardamom
1 teaspoon pure vanilla extract
   or ½ teaspoon vanilla bean
   powder
icing/confectioners' sugar,
   sifted, to decorate (optional)

assortment of small
   bauble- and/or snowflake-
   shaped cutters
2 large baking sheets,
   greased and lined with
   baking parchment
large round icing nozzle/tip
thin ribbon or string/twine

Makes 40

In a large mixing bowl, whisk/beat together the flour, almonds, baking powder, sugar, salt, butter, egg yolk, ground cardamom and vanilla, until the dough is soft and everything is well mixed. Wrap in clingfilm/plastic wrap and chill in the fridge for an hour.

Preheat the oven to 180°C (350°F) Gas 4.

On a flour-dusted surface, roll out the dough to about 5 mm/¼ inch thick and cut out small bauble shapes or any other festive shapes you like. Place on the baking sheets and bake for 8–10 minutes until crisp.

As soon as you remove the cookies from the oven, use a large round icing nozzle/tip to stamp two holes in each cookie to thread the ribbon through. It is important to do this while the cookies are still warm, otherwise the dough will be too fragile to cut. You can cut the holes before baking, but you will need to make them large as the dough will expand a little on baking which can make the holes too small to thread the ribbon through. Leave to cool.

Once cool, thread the ribbon or string/twine through the cookies, placing them an even distance apart. Dust the cookies with icing/confectioners' sugar, if you like, using a doily to create a pretty pattern. Use the cookie ribbons as decoration.

The cookies will store for up to 5 days in an airtight container.

Stained Glass Cookies

Making stained glass cookies is a family tradition for me. They
have such a pretty effect against some twinkling lights. You can
use any boiled sweets/hard candy you like.

115 g/1 stick butter, softened
60 g/5 tablespoons caster/
  superfine sugar
170 g/1¼ cups plain/all-purpose
  flour, sifted, plus extra
  for dusting
10 g/⅓ oz. freeze-dried
  raspberry powder
  (or freeze-dried raspberry
  pieces blitzed to a powder
  in a food processor)
grated zest of 1 lemon
pink food colouring gel
a little milk, if needed
10 clear fruit boiled sweets/
  hard candies

*assortment of star- or
  snowflake-shaped cutters
2 baking sheets, lined with
  silicon mats
large round icing nozzle/tip
ribbon*

Makes 15

Cream together the butter and sugar until soft and creamy.
Sift in the flour, then add the raspberry powder, lemon zest and
a little of the food colouring. Whisk/beat until you have a soft
pink dough. If the dough is too crumbly, add a little milk. Wrap
the dough in clingfilm/plastic wrap and chill in the fridge for
at least 30 minutes.

Preheat the oven to 180°C (350°F) Gas 4.

On a flour-dusted surface, roll out the dough to about
5 mm/¼ inch thick and cut out about 15 cookies. Transfer them
to the baking sheets. When on the baking sheet, cut out shapes
from the centre of each cookie. Re-roll the dough as necessary
and cut out cookies until all the dough is used. Using the icing
nozzle/tip, cut out a large hole near the top of each cookie for
the ribbon to thread through after baking.

Blitz the boiled sweets/hard candies to a fine dust in a food
processor and then spoon the sugar dust into the holes on each
cookie. Depending on how large the holes are that you make,
you may need a few more sweets/hard candies. Bake in the
preheated oven for 10–12 minutes, watching carefully towards
the end so that the sugar does not start to burn. It will have
small bubbles, but do not worry as most of these will disappear
on cooling. Remove from the oven and leave the cookies to cool
on the baking sheets so that the sugar glass sets firm. Once
cool, thread ribbon through the holes and hang them.

The cookies will store for up to 3 days in an airtight container.

Iced Star Cookies

These well-flavoured cookies are simple to make and are ideal decorations. Pick your favourite cookie cutters, then once they are baked, have fun icing and finishing.

150 g/1¼ sticks unsalted butter, softened
100 g/½ cup caster/superfine sugar
finely grated zest and freshly squeezed juice of 1 lemon
75 g/⅓ cup full-fat cream cheese
300 g/2¼ cups plain/all-purpose flour, sifted
a good pinch of salt
1 teaspoon mixed/apple pie spice

FOR THE DECORATION
Royal or Glacé Icing (see page 16), or writing icing pens
edible silver balls

star-shaped cutter
2–3 baking sheets
large round icing nozzle/tip
ribbons

Makes about
24 x 10-cm/ 4-inch stars

Whisk/beat together the butter, sugar and lemon zest using a hand-held electric whisk until soft and creamy. Whisk/beat in 2 teaspoons of the lemon juice and all of the cream cheese. Sift in the flour, salt and mixed/apple pie spice and whisk/beat again. When thoroughly combined, remove the dough from the bowl, shape into a ball and wrap in clingfilm/plastic wrap. Chill in the fridge for about 30 minutes, until firm. The dough can be kept in the fridge, tightly wrapped, for up to 1 week.

Preheat the oven to 180°C (350°F) Gas 4.

On a flour-dusted surface, roll out the dough to about 5 mm/¼ inch thick. Cut out star shapes from the dough, re-rolling as necessary. Place on the baking sheets, leaving space between them. Using the icing nozzle/tip, cut out a large hole near the top of each cookie for the ribbon to thread through after baking.

Bake in the preheated oven for 12–15 minutes until just turning golden brown at the edges. Remove from the oven, leave to cool for 3 minutes, then transfer to a wire rack to cool completely. Decorate with royal or glacé icing, or use a writing icing pen. Stick edible silver balls to the icing, and leave to set. Once the icing is firm, thread the cookies with ribbon.

The cookies will store for up to 5 days in an airtight container.

Swedish Ginger Cookies

These are probably the most famous treat to come out of Sweden. This recipe is a quick dough which is easy to roll out so the kids can make lots of festive shapes. Every December, families across Scandinavia will sit around a table with a batch of dough, festive music on, making loads of cookies and baked goods for all the coming Sundays of Advent.

550 g/4¼ cups plain/all-purpose flour, sifted, plus extra for dusting
1 teaspoon bicarbonate of/baking soda
1½ teaspoons ground ginger
1 teaspoon ground cloves
1 tablespoon ground cinnamon
1 teaspoon ground cardamom
½ teaspoon ground allspice
a pinch of salt
100 g/½ cup granulated sugar
100 g/½ cup soft dark brown sugar
150 g/1¼ sticks butter, softened
200 g/⅔ cup golden/light corn syrup
150 ml/⅔ cup double/heavy cream
Royal Icing (see page 16), to decorate (optional)

assortment of festive-shaped cutters
2–3 baking sheets, lined with baking parchment
piping/pastry bag (optional)

Makes 50-70

In a stand mixer fitted with the paddle attachment, mix the flour, bicarbonate of/baking soda, spices, salt and sugars together. Add the rest of the ingredients, and mix until you have an even dough. Shape it into a log and wrap in clingfilm/plastic wrap, and leave to cool in the fridge at least overnight.

Preheat the oven to 200°C (400°F) Gas 6.

On a flour-dusted surface, roll out the dough to about 2 mm/⅛ inch thick) and use cutters to cut your desired shapes. Make sure they are thin cookies. Place them on the lined baking sheets and bake in batches in the preheated oven for 5–6 minutes. The cookies should be a darker shade of brown without being burnt. Remove from the oven and leave to cool before storing in an airtight container.

If you wish, you can decorate the cookies with piped royal icing or for ease use writing icing pens, and create whatever patterns you like on the cooled cookies.

The cookies will store for up to 5 days in an airtight container.

Christmas Tree Gingerbread Cookies

FOR THE COOKIES
250 g/2 cups gluten-free plain/
   all-purpose flour, sifted,
   plus extra for dusting
100 g/1 cup ground almonds
1 teaspoon bicarbonate of/
   baking soda
100 g/¹/₂ cup caster/superfine
   sugar
1 teaspoon ground cinnamon
1 teaspoon ground ginger
1 tablespoon golden/light
   corn syrup
1 tablespoon black treacle/
   molasses
50 g/3 tablespoons butter,
   softened
1 teaspoon pure vanilla extract
1 egg
1 tablespoon icing/
   confectioners' sugar, sifted
1 egg white

FOR THE DECORATION
250 g/2¹/₂ cups royal icing sugar,
   sifted
1 teaspoon pure vanilla extract
gluten-free sugar decorations
edible glitter
green food colouring pen

*2 baking sheets, greased and
   lined with baking parchment*
Christmas tree-shaped cutters
small round piping nozzle/tip
thin ribbons

Makes 18

'Come to my kitchen and share with me, warm gingerbread cookies and cranberry tea' are the words on a sampler that hangs in my kitchen at Christmas. This recipe is gluten-free, to be shared with all friends during the holidays.

Preheat the oven to 180°C (350°F) Gas 4.

Mix together the flour, ground almonds, bicarbonate of/ baking soda, sugar, cinnamon and ginger. Add the syrup, black treacle/molasses, butter, vanilla extract and egg. Whisk/beat together until you have a soft dough, bringing the dough together with your hands once mixed, and dusting with a little more flour if the dough is too sticky.

On a flour-dusted surface, roll out the dough to 5 mm/¹/₄ inch thick. Cut out shapes with the cutters, re-rolling as necessary, and transfer to the baking sheets using a spatula.

Whisk/beat the icing/confectioners' sugar and the egg white together until foamy, then brush over the top of each cookie using a pastry brush. This will prevent the tops of the cookies from cracking during baking and will give the cookies a shiny glaze. Cut a small hole in the top of each cookie using the piping nozzle/tip. Bake in the preheated oven for 10–15 minutes until just firm. Leave to cool on the baking sheets for a few minutes, then transfer to a wire rack to cool completely.

For the icing, mix the royal icing sugar and vanilla extract with about 2¹/₂ tablespoons of water until the icing is thick and holds a peak. Spread the icing onto the cookies using a round-bladed knife, decorate with the sugar decorations and sprinkle with edible glitter. Leave to set. Once set, you can use a food colouring pen to decorate the cookies and thread with ribbon.

The cookies will store for up to 5 days in an airtight container.

Gift Cookies

Mini Gingerbread Houses

Every Christmas, my niece Hunter celebrates her birthday at my house – like me she is a Christmas baby! For her birthday, the 'birthday fairies' always make her a wintery gingerbread house.

125 g/9 tablespoons butter
100 g/¹/₂ cup caster/superfine sugar
3 heaped tablespoons dark treacle/molasses
300 g/2¹/₄ cups plain/ all-purpose flour, sifted, plus extra for dusting
1 teaspoon bicarbonate of/ baking soda
2 teaspoons ground ginger
1 teaspoon pure vanilla extract or ¹/₂ teaspoon vanilla bean powder
400 g/scant 3 cups royal icing/ confectioners' sugar, sifted
sprinkles and sugar crystals

2 large baking sheets, lined with baking parchment
9-cm/3¹/₂-inch round cutter
gingerbread house templates: 3-cm/1¹/₄-inch square; 2.5-cm/1-inch square; and an end panel with pointed roof that is 2.5-cm/1-inch square, but raising to 4 cm/1¹/₂ inches at the roof point
piping/pastry bag, fitted with a small round nozzle/tip

Makes 8

Preheat the oven to 180°C (350°F) Gas 4.

In a saucepan, heat the butter, sugar and treacle over a gentle heat until the butter has melted. Sift the flour, bicarbonate of/ baking soda and ginger into a mixing bowl. Whisk/beat in the butter mixture and vanilla. The dough will be very soft and warm. Transfer to a cool bowl and leave for about 30 minutes. The dough should become more firm as it cools.

On a flour-dusted surface, roll the dough to 5 mm/¹/₄ inch thick and cut out eight circles using the cutter. Re-roll, and cut out 16 of each template to make the gingerbread house pieces.

Place the gingerbread on the baking sheets and bake in the preheated oven for 8–10 minutes until the gingerbread is firm. Leave the gingerbread to cool completely on a wire rack.

Whisk/beat the icing/confectioners' sugar with 3 tablespoons of water, until you have a smooth, thick icing that holds a peak. Spoon the icing into the piping/pastry bag and pipe windows and doors onto the wall panels of gingerbread.

The icing will dry quite quickly, so assemble one cookie at a time. Add a little icing to one of the round cookies and press one gingerbread panel with the pointed roof into the centre of the cookie. Pipe icing around all the edges of the panel and then press the two side panels into the icing so that they attach to the front of the house. Repeat with the back panel. Pipe icing around the top of the house and press on the roof panels. Pipe a row of icing where the top panels join to seal the roof. Decorate with pretty patterns. Repeat with the remaining houses.

The cookies will store for up to 3 days in an airtight container.

Chocolate Chip Cookies

These giant gluten-free chocolate chip cookies will put a smile on everyone's face. Delicious with a glass of ice-cold milk, packed full of dark and white chocolate, they are a classic cookie for a reason. To keep these gluten-free, check that the chocolate you use does not contain skimmed milk powder as this can contain gluten.

125 g/9 tablespoons butter, softened
125 g/²/₃ cup caster/superfine sugar
125 g/¹/₂ cup dark soft brown sugar
150 g/1 cup plus 2 tablespoons gluten-free plain/all-purpose baking flour, sifted
1 teaspoon bicarbonate of/ baking soda
100 g/1 cup ground almonds
1 egg
60 ml/¹/₄ cup buttermilk
100 g/3¹/₂ oz. dark/bittersweet chocolate, chopped
100 g/3¹/₂ oz. white chocolate buttons

2 baking sheets, greased and lined with baking parchment

Makes about 20

Preheat the oven to 180°C (350°F) Gas 4.

Cream together the butter and both sugars until light and creamy. Add the flour, bicarbonate of/baking soda, ground almonds, egg and buttermilk and whisk/beat until everything is incorporated. Mix in the dark/bittersweet chocolate and white chocolate buttons with a wooden spoon.

Put 20 tablespoonfuls of the mixture on the prepared baking sheets, leaving space between them. (You may need to bake in batches depending on the size of your baking sheets.)

Bake in the preheated oven for 10–12 minutes until golden brown. Leave to cool on the baking sheets for a few minutes then transfer to a wire rack to cool completely.

The cookies will store for up to 5 days in an airtight container.

Wrapped Sweetie Cookies

These pretty swirled cookies are inspired by one of my favourite childhood literary heroes, Willy Wonka, the maker of magical candy! Wrapped in waxed paper they look just like your favourite candies, and are great presented as a gift. It is important to chill the dough well before baking to get the best swirled effect.

125 g/9 tablespoons butter, softened
170 g/generous ¾ cup caster/superfine sugar
1 UK large/US extra-large egg
1 teaspoon pure vanilla extract or ½ teaspoon vanilla bean powder
225 g/1¾ cups plain/all-purpose flour, sifted, plus extra for dusting
1 teaspoon baking powder
pink food colouring gel

2 baking sheets, greased and lined with baking parchment
24 small pieces of waxed paper
ribbons or string/twine

Makes 24

Whisk/beat together the butter and sugar until light and creamy. Whisk/beat in the egg, and then whisk/beat in the vanilla, flour and baking powder until you have a soft dough.

Divide the dough in two and colour one piece with a few drops of pink food colouring gel, mixing in well so that the dough is an even colour. If the dough if too soft to handle, add a little more flour. Wrap the doughs in clingfilm/plastic wrap and chill in the fridge for an hour.

On a flour-dusted surface, roll out the plain dough into a rectangle (30 x 15 cm/12 x 6 inches) and place on a sheet of baking parchment, lifting carefully using the rolling pin to help you. Next roll out the pink dough to the same size and thickness, and place on top of the plain dough, pressing down gently with your hands. Starting from one of the long sides, roll the dough up in a tight spiral so that you end up with a long sausage shape of dough. Wrap in clingfilm/plastic wrap again and chill in the freezer for a further 30 minutes so that the dough is really firm.

Preheat the oven to 180°C (350°F) Gas 4.

Unwrap the dough and, using a sharp knife, slice the dough into 1-cm/³⁄8-inch discs. Place on the baking sheets, leaving space between them. Bake in the preheated oven for 10–12 minutes, then leave to cool completely on the baking sheets.

Wrap each cookie in a piece of waxed paper and tie the ends with ribbon or string/twine, so that they look like giant candies.

The cookies will store for up to 3 days in an airtight container.

Peppermint Bark

Peppermint bark is one of the most traditional American Christmas candies – sheets of peppermint-flavoured chocolate topped with candy cane sprinkles. These cookies are inspired by these! They are made using a clever 'bark press' which is readily available in cake decorating stores or to order online (see page 142), but you can create a bark pattern using the tines of a fork.

115 g/1 stick butter, softened
60 g/5 tablespoons caster/
superfine sugar
140 g/generous 1 cup plain/
all-purpose flour, sifted,
plus extra for dusting
3 tablespoons unsweetened
cocoa powder, sifted
1 tablespoon milk, if needed
100 g/3¹/₂ oz. white chocolate,
broken into small pieces
1 teaspoon peppermint extract
2 tablespoons crushed sugar
candy canes

2 baking sheets, greased and
lined with baking parchment
bark-textured cookie press
(optional)

Makes 12

Preheat the oven to 180°C (350°F) Gas 4.

Whisk/beat together the butter and caster/superfine sugar until light and creamy. Add the flour and cocoa and whisk/beat together to make a soft dough. If the mixture is too crumbly, add a little milk. On a flour-dusted surface, roll out the dough to 5 mm/¹/₄ inch thick and then cut out fingers of cookie dough about 12 x 3 cm/5 x 1¹/₄ inches in size.

Using a spatula, carefully lift the cookie shapes onto the baking sheets. Press the bark press into the dough to make a bark pattern. If you do not have a bark press, make bark patterns in the dough by scraping it gently with the tines of a fork.

Bake in the preheated oven for 10–12 minutes until the cookies are just firm. Leave to cool on the baking sheets for 5 minutes, then move to a wire rack to cool completely.

Melt the white chocolate in a heatproof bowl resting over a pan of simmering water. Stir in the peppermint extract. Dip the end of each cooled cookie in the melted chocolate and then sprinkle each with the crushed candy canes. Place on a sheet of baking parchment and leave in a cool place to set.

The cookies will store for up to 5 days in an airtight container. It is best to store the cookies flat, in single layers, and between sheets of baking parchment.

Christmas Kisses

Hershey's kisses are a popular American candy which come in a wide variety of flavours. They make a perfect filling for small cookie cups, looking pretty with no effort at all. I have used their Candy Cane Flavoured kisses here, as these have pretty red and white stripes. If you do not have Hershey's kisses, you can used other bite-size chocolate candies of your choice to fill the cookie cups. You can use a simple round fluted edge cookie cutter or try a snowflake one, for a more ornate finish.

115 g/1 stick butter, softened
60 g/5 tablespoons soft
dark brown sugar
170 g/1¼ cups plain/all-purpose
flour, sifted, plus extra
for dusting
24 Hershey's candy cane
flavoured kisses, or similar
chocolates
red and white sugar sprinkles
(optional)

5-cm/2-inch round fluted cutter
24-hole mini muffin pan, well
greased

Makes 24

Cream together the butter and sugar until light and creamy. Sift in the flour and whisk/beat in until you have a soft dough. Wrap in clingfilm/plastic wrap and chill in the fridge for 30 minutes.

Preheat the oven to 180°C (350°F) Gas 4.

On a flour-dusted surface, roll out the dough to about 5 mm/¼ inch thick and cut out 24 circles with the cutter, re-rolling as necessary. Press the circles gently into the holes of the mini muffin pan. Bake in the preheated oven for 10–12 minutes until golden and crisp. The dough will puff up slightly but will keep an indent in the centre.

Remove the cookies from the pan. They should pop out easily but you can use a teaspoon to slide them out if they are stuck. Place on a wire rack and, whilst the cookies are still warm, unwrap the Hershey's kisses and place one in the indent of each cookie. Sprinkle with the sugar sprinkles, if you wish, and leave to cool before serving.

The cookies will store for up to 5 days in an airtight container.

Polka-dot Parcels

These colourful parcels make a lovely Christmas gift. Once you have learnt to make the icing bows (see page 21), you can use them on all sorts of different cakes and cookies. If you don't have time to make fondant bows, simply cover the cookies with rolled fondant and tie real ribbons around them.

Gingerbread Cookie Dough (see page 14) or Vanilla Cookie Dough (see page 15)
icing/confectioners' sugar, for dusting
200 g/7 oz. white rolled fondant
200 g/7 oz. red rolled fondant
edible glue

square cutter

Makes 12

Prepare and bake your chosen cookie dough using a square-shaped cutter.

Dust a clean work surface with icing/confectioners' sugar. Make some polka-dot rolled fondant using the technique on page 20. Cut out squares of rolled fondant the same size as the cookies.

Cover the cookies with the polka-dot rolled fondant, following the steps on page 20. Roll out some more red rolled fondant to 3 mm/1/8 inch thick and cut strips of icing about 1 cm/3/8 inches wide. Attach 2 strips to each cookie to make the ribbons.

Make the red fondant bows using the technique on page 21.

Attach the ribbon tails to the middle of the cookies and stick the bows on top to serve, or store in an airtight container, flat, in single layers, between sheets of baking parchment.

For the best results, assemble the cookies with the fondant just before serving.

Name Place Card Cookies

If you are hosting a Christmas Day dinner or a festive supper party, then these peppermint place cards make a unique decoration for your guest table settings. Not only do they look pretty, but they are the perfect accompaniment to coffee at the end of your meal! You can even make a stand for them, by tying three candy canes together, curl-side down.

115 g/1 stick butter, softened
**60 g/5 tablespoons caster/
 superfine sugar**
**170 g/1¼ cups plain/all-purpose
 flour, sifted, plus extra
 for dusting**
**a few drops of peppermint
 extract**
**1 teaspoon pure vanilla extract
 or ½ teaspoon vanilla bean
 powder**
a little milk, if needed
**50 g/2 oz. dark/bittersweet
 chocolate, broken into small
 pieces**
**crushed candy canes or sugar
 crystal cake sprinkles**

*baking sheet, lined with
 baking parchment*
*8-cm/3¼-inch rectangular
 fluted cutter*
*piping/pastry bag, fitted with
 a small round nozzle/tip*

Makes 10

Cream together the butter and sugar and then sift in the flour and mix until you have a soft dough. Add the peppermint and vanilla extract. If the dough is too crumbly, add a little milk. Wrap the dough in clingfilm/plastic wrap and chill in the fridge for at least 30 minutes.

Preheat the oven to 180°C (350°F) Gas 4.

Roll out the dough on a flour-dusted surface to 5 mm/¼ inch thick. Cut out 10 cookies, re-rolling as necessary. Transfer to the baking sheet using a spatula and bake for 10–15 minutes until lightly golden brown. Leave to cool on the baking sheet for a few minutes, then transfer to a wire rack to cool completely.

Place the chocolate in a bowl resting over a pan of simmering water until the chocolate melts. Leave to cool for a short while so that the chocolate cools but is still runny, then spoon into the piping/pastry bag. Pipe a rectangle of chocolate around the edge of the cookie for the border and sprinkle it with crushed candy canes or sugar crystals to decorate, tipping away any excess. Pipe the names of your guests in the centre of each cookie with the remaining chocolate. Leave to cool so that the chocolate sets or if you're in a hurry, chill them in the fridge.

The cookies will store for up to 3 days in an airtight container.

Advent Numbered Cookies

You will need a selection of numbered cookie cutters, preferably in different sizes, and plain cutters in different shapes to make these. Present them to friends and family so they can celebrate Advent.

FOR THE VANILLA SHORTBREAD
225 g/2 sticks butter, softened
250 g/1¾ cups plus
    2 tablespoons plain/
    all-purpose flour, sifted,
    plus extra for dusting
½ teaspoon salt
75 g/½ cup icing/confectioners'
    sugar, sifted
1 teaspoon pure vanilla extract

FOR THE CHOCOLATE
    SHORTBREAD
225 g/2 sticks butter, softened
200 g/1½ cups plain/all-purpose
    flour, sifted
50 g/½ cup unsweetened
    cocoa powder
½ teaspoon salt
75 g/½ cup icing/confectioners'
    sugar, sifted
1 teaspoon pure vanilla extract

assortment of cutters, e.g.
    round, square and oval,
    plus numbered cutters
2 baking sheets, lined
    with baking parchment
24 cellophane bags

Makes about 24

To make the vanilla shortbread, whisk/beat the butter in a mixing bowl with a wooden spoon until smooth and very soft. Meanwhile, sift together the flour and salt. Add the icing/confectioners' sugar to the creamed butter and continue mixing until light and fluffy. Add the vanilla and mix again. Add the sifted flour and salt and mix until it starts to come together into a dough.

To knead the dough, first sprinkle a little flour on a clean work surface. Then shape the dough into a ball and push on it and press it onto the work surface, turning it round often.

Do this for a minute, then flatten into a disc, cover with clingfilm/plastic wrap and chill until needed.

To make the chocolate shortbread, follow the steps as above, but add the cocoa powder to the flour and salt.

Preheat the oven to 180°C (350°F) Gas 4.

On a flour-dusted surface, roll out the doughs (separately) to 2–3 mm/⅛ inch thick and cut out 24 shapes using the assorted cutters. Arrange on the prepared baking sheets. Using the numbered cutters, stamp out numbers 1–24 and stick to each larger cookie with a dab of cold water. Leave the cookies to chill in the fridge for 10 minutes.

Bake in batches on the middle shelf of the preheated oven for about 10–12 minutes, or until firm and starting to go crisp at the edges.

Remove from the oven and leave to cool on the sheets before packaging into cellophane bags as gifts, if you like.

Danish Vanilla Cookies

Around the world, people buy Danish butter cookies in pretty tins, but those cookies taste nothing like these home-made ones – these are so much better and make a perfect gift for the holiday season.

1 whole vanilla pod/bean
250 g/1¼ cups caster/superfine sugar
250 g/2¼ sticks cold butter, cubed
325 g/scant 2½ cups plain/ all-purpose flour, sifted
a pinch of salt
1 teaspoon baking powder
75 g/²/₃ cup ground almonds
1 egg
50 g/¼ cup finely chopped almonds

3–4 baking sheets, greased and lined with baking parchment
piping/pastry bag, fitted with a large star nozzle/tip

Makes 40

Grind the whole vanilla pod/bean, including the skin, with 3 tablespoons of the caster/superfine sugar in a spice grinder or food processor. Sift out any big lumps and set aside.

In a stand mixer or food processor, combine the cold butter with the plain/all-purpose flour, salt, baking powder and the vanilla sugar mixture. Mix with the paddle attachment or pulse briefly, until the mixture has a coarse, sandy texture.

Add the ground almonds and remaining caster/superfine sugar and mix again, then add the egg and chopped almonds. Mix until you have an even dough that is soft enough to push through a piping/pastry bag. It may help to warm the dough with your hands until mouldable. Alternatively, you can also simply roll these, but they will not have the pattern.

Pipe (or roll) the dough into 8–10 cm/3¼–4 inch long sausages. Carefully connect the two ends of each to form rings and place on the baking sheets, leaving space between them.

Chill the dough rings on the baking sheets in the fridge for at least 30 minutes. This will help the cookies to keep their piped pattern as they bake.

Preheat the oven to 200°C (400°F) Gas 6.

Bake in the preheated oven for 8–10 minutes, or until the edges are just golden brown. Remove from the oven and leave to cool and harden before eating. Store in an airtight container as the cookies do go soft quickly.

'With Love' Custard Creams

A sweet winter gift, you can eat the custard cream filling first, then dunk the cookie into a hot mug of tea, coffee or cocoa. The passion fruit powder boosts the flavour nicely.

FOR THE COOKIES
200 g/1³⁄₄ stick butter, softened
125 g/scant 1 cup icing/
   confectioners' sugar
1 teaspoon pure vanilla extract
2 eggs
300 g/2¹⁄₃ cups plain/all-purpose
   flour, plus extra for dusting
¹⁄₂ teaspoon baking powder
50 g/¹⁄₂ cup custard/instant
   pudding powder
30 g/2 tablespoons freeze-dried
   passion fruit powder
a pinch of salt

FOR THE BUTTERCREAM
125 g/4¹⁄₂ oz. white chocolate
2 large passion fruit, flesh
   scooped out, skins discarded
125 g/9 tablespoons butter,
   softened
70 g/scant ³⁄₄ cup icing/
   confectioners' sugar
¹⁄₂ teaspoon pure vanilla extract
1 teaspoon freeze-dried passion
   fruit powder

*2 large baking sheets, greased
   and lined with baking
   parchment*
mini heart-shaped cutter
'with love' cookie stamp

Makes 18

For the cookies, cream the butter and sugar together until pale and light. Add the vanilla and mix again. Gradually whisk/beat in the eggs. Sift in the flour, baking powder, custard and passion fruit powders, and salt, and whisk/beat until smooth. On a flour-dusted surface, bring the dough together into a ball. Wrap in clingfilm/plastic wrap, and chill for at least 4 hours.

Preheat the oven to 170°C (325°F) Gas 3.

On a flour-dusted surface, roll out half the dough to 2 mm/¹⁄₈ inch thick. Cut out as many cookies as you can, re-rolling as necessary, and arrange on the baking sheets. Stamp half the cookies with the stamp and bake on the middle shelf of the preheated oven for 12 minutes, or until crisp. Remove from the oven and leave the cookies to cool slightly on the baking sheets before transferring to a wire rack to cool completely.

For the buttercream, break the chocolate into pieces and melt in a heatproof bowl set over a saucepan of barely simmering water. Stir gently until the chocolate has melted and the mixture is smooth. Remove from the heat and set aside to cool.

Press the passion fruit pulp and juice through a fine mesh sieve/strainer set over a bowl, discarding the black seeds. Cream together the butter, sugar, vanilla, passion fruit pulp and passion fruit powder using a hand-held electric whisk until smooth and very light. Mix into the cooled white chocolate.

Spread the underside of the unstamped cookies with buttercream, then top with the stamped cookies.

The cookies will store for up to 3 days in an airtight container.

Apple Cinnamon Sugar Cookies

180 g/1½ cups gluten-free
   self-raising/self-rising flour,
   sifted
180 g/1¾ cups ground almonds
150 g/¾ cup demerara/
   turbinado sugar
1 teaspoon bicarbonate of/
   baking soda
1 teaspoon ground cinnamon
150 g/1 cup cinnamon-flavoured
   mixed sultanas/golden raisins
   and dried apple pieces (or
   plain mixed sultanas/golden
   raisins and dried apple pieces)
125 g/9 tablespoons butter
2 tablespoons golden/light
   corn syrup
1 egg
pearl or nibbed sugar, to sprinkle

*2 large baking sheets, greased
   and lined with baking
   parchment*

Makes 12

Apple and cinnamon are two of my favourite flavours
at Christmas. These are gluten-free and great to serve
with mulled wine on a chilly evening. The pearl sugar
adds crunch to the cookies, and looks like snow.

Preheat the oven to 180°C (350°F) Gas 4.

Put the flour, ground almonds, demerara/turbinado sugar,
bicarbonate of/baking soda, ground cinnamon and dried fruit
in a mixing bowl, and stir together so that they are well mixed.

Heat the butter with the syrup in a saucepan over low heat
until the butter has melted. Leave to cool slightly, then stir into
the dry ingredients with a wooden spoon. Beat in the egg to
form a dough that is soft but not sticky.

Place 12 large balls of the dough on the prepared baking
sheets, leaving space between them, and press down slightly
with clean fingers. Sprinkle the pearl sugar over the top of the
cookies and bake for 12–15 minutes, until golden brown.

Remove from the oven and leave to cool on the baking sheets
for a few minutes, then transfer to a wire rack with a spatula to
cool completely.

The cookies will store for up to 5 days in an airtight container.

Chocolate Chip Biscotti

Crisp, crunchy chocolate Italian biscotti studded with chunks of dark chocolate and pecans – lovely with ice cream as well as hot drinks in the winter.

3 UK large/US extra-large eggs
200 g/1¼ cups light brown muscovado sugar
finely grated zest of 1 orange
115 g/1 stick butter, melted
325 g/2⅓ cups plain/all-purpose flour, sifted, plus extra for dusting
1 tablespoon baking powder
25 g/¼ cup unsweetened cocoa powder
100 g/1 cup pecan pieces
100 g/3½ oz. dark/bittersweet chocolate, coarsely chopped

2 baking sheets, lined with baking parchment

Makes about 36

Preheat the oven to 180°C (350°F) Gas 4.

Put the eggs, sugar and orange zest in a large mixing bowl and whisk/beat with a hand-held electric whisk until very frothy. Whisk/beat in the melted butter. Sift the flour, baking powder and cocoa into the bowl and mix with a wooden spoon. Mix in the pecans and chopped chocolate until thoroughly combined.

On a flour-dusted surface, divide the dough into 2 equal portions. Using well-floured hands, lift a portion of dough onto each prepared sheet and shape into a brick of about 30 x 7 cm/ 12 x 3 inches as they will spread in the oven. Bake in the preheated oven for 25–30 minutes until just firm. Turn off the oven and remove the sheets and leave to cool completely.

When ready to continue, reheat the oven to 180°C (350°F) Gas 4. Using a serrated bread knife, slice the logs (still on the sheets) on the diagonal about 1 cm/³/8 inch thick. Put, cut-side down, on the sheets and return to the oven. Bake for 10 minutes until crisp and dry.

Remove the sheets from the oven, transfer to a wire rack and leave to cool completely.

The biscotti will store for up to 3 weeks in an airtight container.

Swedish Pepper Cookies

200 g/1¹/₂ cups plain/
   all-purpose flour, sifted,
   plus extra for dusting
¹/₂ teaspoon bicarbonate of/
   baking soda
1 teaspoon ground cinnamon
1 teaspoon ground ginger
¹/₂ teaspoon ground
   black pepper
grated zest of 1 orange
150 g/³/₄ cup caster/superfine
   sugar
115 g/1 stick butter, chilled
   and diced
1 egg
1 tablespoon black treacle/
   molasses

star-shaped cutter
3 baking sheets, greased

Makes about 15

Traditionally made for the Christmas holidays, these dark spicy cookies can be left plain or decorated with white icing – you can use ready-made icing writing pens for this.

Put all the ingredients in a food processor and blend until the mixture forms a soft dough.

When thoroughly combined, remove the dough from the processor, shape into a ball and wrap in clingfilm/plastic wrap. Chill in the fridge until firm for about 1 hour.

Remove the dough from the fridge, unwrap and roll out on a lightly floured work surface until about 5 mm/¹/₄ inch thick. Dip the cookie cutter in flour and cut out shapes, re-rolling as necessary. Arrange the cookies on the baking sheets, leaving space between them, and chill in the fridge for 10 minutes.

Preheat the oven to 160°C (325°F) Gas 3.

Bake in the preheated oven for 10–12 minutes until dark golden brown and firm. Remove from the oven and leave to cool for 5 minutes, then transfer to a wire rack to cool completely.

The cookies will store for up to 1 week in an airtight container.

Lebkuchen

In Germany, Christmas just wouldn't be Christmas without lebkuchen. Traditionally, they are made from honey and seven spices, but this delicious version is based on meringue and nuts and with just six spices – crisp and light but densely flavoured.

100 g/¾ cup almonds
(not blanched)
25 g/1 oz. dark/bittersweet
chocolate, coarsely chopped
2 tablespoons mixed candied
peel, very finely chopped
½ teaspoon ground cinnamon
½ teaspoon ground ginger
¼ teaspoon freshly grated
nutmeg
¼ teaspoon ground
black pepper
¼ teaspoon ground cloves
¼ teaspoon ground allspice
2 UK large/US extra-large
egg whites
115 g/1 cup icing/confectioners'
sugar, sifted

TO DECORATE
150 g/7 oz. good dark/
bittersweet chocolate,
chopped

*3 baking sheets, lined
with baking parchment*

Makes 16

Preheat the oven to 150°C (300°F) Gas 2.

Put the almonds and chopped chocolate into the a food processor and process until the mixture looks like fine crumbs. Mix with the finely chopped peel and all the spices.

Put the egg whites into a clean, grease-free bowl and, using a hand-held electric whisk or mixer, whisk/beat until stiff peaks form. Gradually whisk/beat in the icing/confectioners' sugar, then whisk/beat for another minute to make a very stiff, glossy meringue. Sprinkle the spice mixture over the top and gently fold in with a large spoon.

Take tablespoons of the mixture and drop them on the prepared baking sheets, leaving space between them. Using a round-bladed knife, spread out each mound to a disc of about 7 cm/3 inches in diameter. Bake in the preheated oven for 15–20 minutes, until pale gold and firm.

Remove from the oven and leave to cool completely on the baking sheet. When cooled, peel the lebkuchen off the baking parchment and set on a wire rack.

To decorate, melt the chocolate in a heatproof bowl set over a pan of simmering water. Stir gently until melted, then remove from the heat. Spread some melted chocolate over one side of each lebkuchen with a palette knife or metal spatuka, then leave to set on a sheet of baking parchment.

The cookies will store for up to 4 days in an airtight container.

Index

(Page numbers in *italic* refer to photographs)

Stockists and Suppliers

UK:

Cake Stuff
www.cake-stuff.com
Online-only stockist of cookie decorating supplies, from festive cookie cutters and decorative accessories, to edibles such as Christmas tree sprinkles, food colouring gels and much more.

The Vanilla Valley Cake and Baking Equipment
www.thevanillavalley.co.uk
Cookie decorating supplies and equipment for professionals and hobby bakers, including edibles, festive gift bags and boxes.

Sugar Shack
www.sugarshack.co.uk
Christmas baking equipment, including plenty of cookie cutters, such as gingerbread, snowflakes and baubles, and edible icing sheets and printers (see page 74).

Global Sugar Art
www.globalsugarart.com
Stockists of food coloring gels, metallic food paints and fondant icing in a range of colours, as well as other cookie making supplies.

Kenwood
www.kenwoodworld.com
Manufacturers and suppliers of the iconic Kenwood mixer.

The Cake Decorating Company
www.thecakedecoratingcompany.co.uk
Large variety of products for gift baking from treat bags and rubber stamps, to templates and festive cookie moulds and cutters.

Hobbycraft
www.hobbycraft.co.uk
Arts and crafts store with plenty of inspiration for Christmas table decorations and cookie displays.

Fantastic Ribbons
www.fantasticribbons.com
Leading stockist of decorative ribbons, perfect for wrapping your cookie swap gifts.

Lakeland
www.lakeland.co.uk
A wide range of general kitchen and baking equipment, plus cookie decorating supplies.

John Lewis
www.johnlewis.com
Department store stocking seasonal items, quality bakeware and other branded appliances.

US:

Global Sugar Art
www.globalsugarart.com
Cookie making supplies and edible sugar decorating candies.

NYCake
www.NYcake.com
Stockists of cookie making supplies, from cutters, pans and decorative packaging, to edible sprinkles, glitter and food colouring gels.

Squires Kitchen Shop
www.squires-shop.com
For good-quality sugar pastes in a wide range of colours plus sugar paste cutters. Stockists of Wilton products in the UK (see listing below).

Wilton
www.wilton.com
Huge range of cookie supplies, including an online video gallery of piping and other icing techniques.

Ink 4 Cakes
www.ink4cakes.com
Large supplier of edible icing sheets and printers (see page 74).

Crate&Barrel
www.crateandbarrel.com
Homeware store for festive and contemporary bakeware, and other lifestyle brand kitchen appliances.

Sur La Table
www.surlatable.com
Stocks a good range of general baking equipment and kitchenware, from cookie cutters to piping bags, perfect for hobby bakers.

Recipe Credits

Hannah Miles
Apple and Cinnamon
    Sugar Cookies
Candy Cane Cookies
Carrots for Rudolf
Chocolate Chip Cookies
Christmas Kisses
Christmas Pudding Cookies
Christmas Tree
    Gingerbread Cookies
Clementine Linzer
    Sandwiches
Coconut Snowballs
Coffee Cookies with
    Vintage Edible Transfers
Frosted Pine Cones
Garland Cookies
Gingerbread Viennese
    Whirl Sandwich Cookies
Gingerbread Whoopie Pies
Hot Chocolate Cups with
    Candy Cane Handles
Iced Mitten Cookies
Meringue Snowmen
    Cookies
Mini Gingerbread Houses
Name Place Card Cookies
Peppermint Bark
Polar Bear Snow Globes
Red Velvet Snowcaps
Reindeer Cookies
Santa Cookies
Snow Scene Cookies
Snowcap Cookies
Snowflake Cookies
Snowmen Faces
Stained Glass Cookies
Sugar Sprinkle Stars
Treacle House Cookies

Walnut Cookies
Wrapped Sweetie Cookies
Wreath Cookies

Annie Rigg
Advent Numbered Cookies
Almond Crescents
Christmas Stars
Frosted Snowflakes
Gingerbread Cookie Dough
Icing Techniques
Santa Claus Gingerbread
Vanilla Cookie Dough

Brontë Aurell
Danish Vanilla Cookies
Ginger Medal Cookies
Nordic Spiced Cookies
Norwegian Butter Cookies
Snowy Peak Cookies
Swedish Ginger Cookies
Toffee Cookie Slices

Linda Collister
Chocolate Chip Biscotti
Iced Star Biscuits
Lebkuchen
Swedish Pepper Cookies

Chloe Coker
Baubles
Jolly Penguins
Polka-dot Parcels

Susannah Blake
Dove Cookies

Will Torrent
'With Love' Custard Creams

Picture Credits

Key: a = above, b = below,
l = left, r = right

Caroline Arber
11, 22al, 22ar, 110ar, 110br,

Carolyn Barber
81

Peter Cassidy
*4, 5, 27, 34, 40, 46, 53, 55, 57,
82ar, 106, 128*

**Kate Davis, James Gardiner
& Claire Richardson**
110bl, 143

Tara Fisher
17, 45, 58bl, 66, 67, 90

Jonathan Gregson
22br, 130

Adrian Lawrence
16, 18

Lisa Linder
22bl, 54, 82br, 126

William Lingwood
3, 44, 87, 99, 136

Martin Norris
*18al, 19, 20, 21, 58br, 70, 82bl,
98, 110al, 122*

Steve Painter
*1, 6, 24, 25, 28, 29, 30, 32, 33,
37, 38, 40, 50, 61, 62, 63, 64,
65, 68, 69, 73, 74, 75, 77, 78,
84, 85, 86, 89, 92, 93, 94, 97,
100, 101, 102, 103, 113, 116, 117,
118, 120, 121, 123, 125, 144*

William Reavell
*9, 12, 41, 48, 49, 80, 105, 109,
114, 128, 132, 133, 134, 137, 138*

Kate Whitaker
2, 52, 58ar

Polly Wreford
58al